W9-BIK-687

Love's Humility

Love's Humility

by
John MacArthur, Jr.

WORD OF GRACE COMMUNICATIONS
P.O. Box 4000
Panorama City, CA 91412

© 1983 by
JOHN MACARTHUR, JR.

Moody Press Edition, 1986

All rights reserved. No part of this book may be reproduced in any form without permission in writing from the publisher, except in the case of brief quotations embodied in critical articles or reviews.

All Scripture quotations, unless noted otherwise, are from the *New Scofield Reference Bible,* King James Version. Copyright © 1967 by Oxford University Press, Inc. Reprinted by permission.

The use of selected references from various versions of the Bible in this publication does not necessarily imply publisher endorsement of the versions in their entirety.

ISBN: 0-8024-5097-0

1 2 3 4 5 6 7 Printing/GB/Year 91 90 89 88 87 86

Printed in the United States of America

Contents

These Bible studies are taken from messages delivered by Pastor-Teacher John MacArthur, Jr., at Grace Community Church in Panorama City, California. These messages have been combined into a 6-tape album entitled *Love's Humility*. You may purchase this series either in an attractive vinyl cassette album or as individual cassettes. To purchase these tapes, request the album *Love's Humility* or ask for the tapes by their individual GC numbers. Please consult the current price list; then, send your order, making your check payable to:

WORD OF GRACE COMMUNICATIONS
P.O. Box 4000
Panorama City, CA 91412

Or, call the following toll-free number:
1-800-55-GRACE

1
An Eye for an Eye—
Part 1

Outline

Introduction
A. The Readiness to Fight for Rights
   1. The mind-set
   2. The misunderstanding
B. The Result of Fighting for Rights
C. The Refusal to Fight for Rights

Lesson
I. The Principle of Mosaic Law
  A. Examining the Principle
    1. Exodus 21
    2. Leviticus 24
    3. Deuteronomy 19
  B. Explaining the Principle
    1. It is a just law
    2. It is a merciful law
    3. It is a beneficial law
  C. Exercising the Principle
    1. Leviticus 19:18
    2. Proverbs 25:21
    3. Proverbs 24:29
II. The Perversion of Jewish Teaching
  A. The Prevailing Pattern
  B. The Proper Perspective

Introduction

A. The Readiness to Fight for Rights

   1. The mind-set

One element of the American philosophy of life is that everyone has certain inalienable rights. Our society is big

1

on rights. We have different movements advocating civil rights, women's rights, children's rights, and prisoners' rights. Unions demand rights for employees. People are so obsessed with rights that it's not uncommon to hear someone say, "You'll never get away with that; I'll get even with you!"

Once when I was driving home with my family, I got onto the freeway and pulled in front of someone a little more closely than he thought I should have. I didn't hit his car, but apparently I dented his psyche. For the next five miles the man followed me, flashing his bright lights and honking his horn. He was demanding his right to a certain area of the freeway on which he allowed no one to infringe.

Deep down in the human heart is a retaliatory spirit, which came about as a result of the curse of sin. That vengeful spirit is in all of us. There's a story about a bride and groom long ago who were leaving on their honeymoon in a buggy pulled by a horse. The horse bolted, and the man said, "That's one!" The horse bolted again, and the groom said, "That's two!" The same thing happened again, and the groom said, "That's three!" He then pulled out his gun and killed the horse. His wife said, "That's terrible; you can't do that!" The husband replied, "That's one!"

In our society, we make heroes out of people who won't take guff from anyone. We idolize people who are strong, tough, courageous, and macho—and look down on those who are meek, gentle, forgiving, and gracious. The merciful person who is not demanding is called a weakling and a coward. I think one reason Americans idolize John Wayne is that he was a symbol of the crusty, take-nothing-from-nobody folk hero who characterizes our society.

2. The misunderstanding

It's part of human nature to want to get even with someone who does something to us that we don't like. That explains the Jewish miscomprehension of the biblical phase "An eye for an eye, and a tooth for a tooth" (Matt. 5:38; cf. Ex. 21:24). The Jewish leaders during Christ's time interpreted that to mean, "Give a person what he is due." They used that principle as a license for vengeance; they considered it biblical permission to have a grudge. However, Christ said, "Whosoever shall smite thee on thy right cheek, turn to him the other also. And if any man will sue thee at the law, and take away thy coat, let him have thy cloak also. And whosoever shall compel thee to go a mile, go with him two. Give to him that asketh thee, and from him that would borrow of thee turn not thou away" (Matt. 5:39-42). What Jesus said is antithetical to everything in human nature.

B. The Result of Fighting for Rights

When a fight for rights takes place in a society, the inevitable result is lawlessness. When people fight for their rights, they act selfishly, and when many people are acting selfishly at once, they will invariably tread on each other. In their selfishness, people will push the law into the background. C. S. Lewis realized that the human heart is characterized by the desire to fight for rights and get even. He used that concept as the basis of his argument for moral law in the universe in *Mere Christianity* [New York: Macmillan, 1977], pp. 17-21).

Everyone has a sense of justice that comes from being created in the image of God (Gen. 1:26), but after the Fall, our sense of justice became perverted into a vengeful spirit. People don't want to correct something for the sake of the law and to glorify God by upholding His standard; they basically want to get even. That's a perversion of the moral righteousness given us in creation. James 4:1 tells about those who have a retaliatory spirit: "From where come wars and fightings among you? Come they not here, [because] of your lusts?" We have war because the normal desire for justice has been perverted into a lust for retaliation. That's why so many people fight for their rights and push aside society's laws. Some parents have said to me, "It's easier to give in to my child's demands than to try to discipline him." Society is saying the same thing.

C. The Refusal to Fight for Rights

Let's contrast the fight for rights with what the apostle Paul says in 1 Corinthians 9:4-6: "Have we no right to eat and to drink? Have we no right to lead about a sister, a wife, as well as other apostles, and as the brethren of the Lord, and Cephas? Or I only, and Barnabas, have we no right to forbear working?" Paul was saying, "I am a minister of the gospel;

3

have I no right to earn a living doing that? Do I have to work to earn my living? Don't I have a right to be paid for my ministry? Don't I have a right to marry and take a sister in Christ to be my wife?" Then he says in verse 12, "Nevertheless, we have not used this right, but bear all things, lest we should hinder the gospel of Christ." Paul set aside his rights for the sake of the gospel. In Romans 14:13-21 and 15:1-3, Paul says we are not to use our Christian liberty to make someone else stumble. We have certain rights, but some of those rights can be offensive to others (such as in Romans 14:21).

Don't push your desire for rights to the point where you obliterate the law. Our Lord addresses that issue in Matthew 5:38-42. There, He contrasts the ethics of His kingdom—forgiveness, lack of selfishness, and lack of self-defensiveness—with the retaliatory spirit that characterizes society.

I have had the opportunity to stand on the Mount of Beatitudes, which is near the place where Jesus spoke the Sermon on the Mount (Matt. 5-7). It is a beautiful green hill dotted with some trees, and it slopes down to a shore on the Sea of Galilee. I've imagined what it must have been like to be there when Jesus taught His sermon. Before Him was a multitude of people. The scribes and Pharisees were probably in the front of the crowd because they thought they were the best of men; Christ's disciples were most likely at His feet.

In the latter part of Matthew 5, Jesus is speaking about the form of religion developed by the scribes and Pharisees. These Jewish religious leaders believed they had attained self-righteousness on their own merit. They believed they were able to enter the kingdom of God on the basis of their own self-righteousness. The scribes and Pharisees had attained a standard of excellence through legalistic laws and rituals, and masked the reality of their sinfulness. Christ ripped off their masks so they would see their own sinfulness. Was that unkind? No; the kindest thing you can do for someone is to show him his sin so he knows he needs a Savior. No one will come to Christ unless he knows he needs Him.

Prior to Matthew 5:38, Christ shows the scribes and Pharisees that they were murderers, adulterers, and liars in spite of what they thought. From Matthew 5:38 on, He shows them that they had vengeful, grudging spirits that were not char-

4

acteristic of citizens in the kingdom of God. He explained God's standard to them, and said that they fell short.

Matthew 5:38 has confused many people. Some people have used that verse to advocate lawlessness, pacifism, conscientious objection, disbelief in capital punishment, and disbelief in justice. Leo Tolstoy, the great nineteenth-century Russian novelist, used the Sermon on the Mount in his book *What I Believe* to defend his belief that if there were no policemen, soldiers, or other authorities, we would be in utopia. That's ridiculous! To better understand Matthew 5:38, we will look at three things: the principle of Mosaic law, the perversion of Jewish teaching, and the perspective of Jesus.

Lesson

I. THE PRINCIPLE OF MOSAIC LAW

In Matthew 5:38 Christ tells the Jewish religious leaders, "Ye have heard that it hath been said, An eye for an eye, and a tooth for a tooth." The phrase "ye have heard that it hath been said" indicates that the law "an eye for an eye, and a tooth for a tooth" was a part of Jewish tradition. The Jewish religious leaders adopted that principle based on the interpretations their rabbis had handed down to them. Christ was quoting an Old Testament principle, but He wanted to point out to the scribes and Pharisees that they had misapplied the principle, as they had many other principles in the Old Testament. As we study what that law meant, keep in mind that lawlessness results when people struggle selfishly for their rights.

Ultimate Law and Order

Matthew 5:38 helps give us a perspective on where society's laws fit in the life of a believer. The Bible upholds law and order. It talks about forgiveness and turning the other cheek, but it is never against doing what is lawful. Throughout the Bible, God exhalts law. He made society to be lawful. Through the minor prophets, God repeatedly indicted the people of Israel for their unjust judges and unlawful acts.

It is essential to have laws. Romans 13:1 says that people who are in positions of authority are "ordained of God." First Timothy 1 explains why God established law: "The law is not made for a righteous man but for the lawless and disobedient, for the

5

ungodly and for sinners, for unholy and profane, for murderers of fathers and murdrers of mothers, for manslayers, for fornicators, for them that defile themselves with mankind [homosexuals]" (vv. 9-10). Notice that in the fight for homosexual rights, many people obviate the law that God ordained to preserve a righteous standard. The law tends to get muddled in a fight for rights because men are evil and the things they want are usually unlawful. First Timothy 1:10-11 explains that the law is given "for kidnapers, for liars, for perjured persons, and . . . any other thing that is contrary to sound doctrine, according to the glorious gospel of the blessed God." God gave the law to protect righteous men from ungodly men. At no time are we to obviate the law.

We are to forgive, turn the other cheek, give to someone who sues us, and give to anyone who wants to borrow from us. But where does legal recourse fit into the picture if someone commits a crime against me? Do I just tell a criminal, "It's all right for you to steal from me. Would you like to take anything else?" Are we to forgive offenders and free them, or should we uphold the law and punish them. Let's find out with a closer look at Matthew 5:38.

A. Examining the Principle

The statement "an eye for an eye, and a tooth for a tooth" is frequently misunderstood. Many think it's a merciless, bloodthirsty Old Testament law. Some critics of the Bible say that the God of the New Testament is not the God of the Old Testament. They say that the God of the Old Testament allowed retaliation: When someone did something to you, it was all right to get him back. People interpret Matthew 5:38 that way because of the sinful state of the human heart. However, that's not the way God's heart is, and the Old Testament is not about a God who is merciless.

In Exodus 20 we find the moral law, which exists between man and God. In Exodus 21-23 we find the civil law, which exists between man and man. God instituted judges, magistrates, and authorities to take care of civil matters.

There are three places in the Old Testament where the law "an eye for an eye, and a tooth for a tooth" appears. In all three places, it relates to civil situations that have to do with a duly constituted authority, such as a judge or a magistrate. In no way is that law related to personal relationships. But that's what the Pharisees had done with it: They had taken a divine principle for the courts and made it a matter of daily

6

vendettas. Let's look at how "an eye for an eye, and a tooth for a tooth" is used in the Old Testament:

1. Exodus 21

   Verse 22 says, "If men strive, and hurt a woman with child, so that her fruit depart from her, and yet no mischief follows; he shall be surely punished, according as the woman's husband will lay upon him; and he shall pay as the judges determine." If a pregnant woman was harmed, regardless of whether the child was lost, her husband had the right to seek damages. A judge was to determine the fine because that was a civil matter. The husband wasn't to get a club and beat up the man who harmed his wife. Exodus 21:22 does not speak of personal vengeance. For there to be structure in law and preservation of society, you can't have personal vengeance.

   Verses 23-27 continue, "If any mischief follows, then thou shalt give life for life, eye for eye, tooth for tooth, hand for hand, foot for foot, burning for burning, wound for wound, stripe for stripe. And if a man smite the eye of his servant, or the eye of his maid, that it perish; he shall let him go free for his eye's sake. And if he smite out his manservant's tooth, or his maidservant's tooth; he shall let him go free for his tooth's sake." Within the framework of civil law, God protected the weak from the strong by establishing just recourse.

   The term "judges" in verse 22 tells us that the phrase "eye for eye, tooth for tooth" in verse 24 has to do with civil law. If a servant's tooth was knocked out by an employer, the servant was not to wait for an opportunity to knock out one of his employer's teeth. He was to go to one of Israel's courts and report what had happened, along with the confirmation of two or three witnesses. If he won the case, he would receive compensation for his injury. That would temper the master's treatment of his slaves. A master didn't want to lose a slave every time he knocked out a slave's tooth; that was a high price to pay. Law is a restraint; when justice is enacted speedily and equitably, it has a great effect on society.

2. Leviticus 24

   Verses 19-20 say, "If a man cause a blemish in his neighbor; as he hath done, so shall it be done to him: Breach for breach, eye for eye, tooth for tooth: as he hath

caused a blemish in a man, so shall it be done to him."
The punishment is to fit the crime. Note that Leviticus 24
is also in a civil setting.

3. Deuteronomy 19

    Here we read, "One witness shall not rise up against a
    man for any iniquity, or for any sin, in any sin that he
    sinneth; at the mouth of two witnesses, or at the mouth
    of three witnesses, shall the matter be established" (v.
    15). You can't convict a man of wrongdoing unless you
    have sufficient witnesses. Verses 16-19 continue, "If a
    false witness rise up against any man to testify against
    him that which is wrong, then both the men, between
    whom the controversy is, shall stand before the Lord,
    before the priests and the judges, who shall be in those
    days; and the judges shall make diligent inquiry; and,
    behold, if the witness be a false witness, and hath
    testified falsely against his brother, then shall ye do unto
    him, as he had thought to have done unto his brother. So
    shalt thou put the evil away from among you." Do you
    want to know how to get rid of evil in society? Speedily
    give just punishment to people who commit crimes,
    including perjury.

    Verses 20-21a say, "Those who remain shall hear, and
    fear, and shall henceforth commit no more any such evil
    among you. And thine eye shall not pity." There is no
    place for pity in a law court. The law demands justice. If
    society is to be preserved, there must be justice. A judge
    once felt sorry for a rapist and let him go. Later on, the
    man raped and murdered a nine-year-old girl. Then the
    judge felt sorry for the little girl. The court is not the place
    for pity upon criminals; it is where the standard of
    righteousness is to be upheld. When a court does that,
    society will be preserved and people will be afraid to
    break the law.

    If you indiscriminately give rights to innately sinful man,
    he will break the law. You must prescribe consequences
    for bad behavior. If parents don't prescribe consequences
    for the bad behavior of their children, the children will
    never learn what it means to live a righteous life. There
    must be consequences; that's why Deuteronomy 19:21
    says, "Life shall go for life, eye for eye, tooth for tooth,
    hand for hand, foot for foot."

The law "an eye for an eye, and a tooth for a tooth" was

clearly intended for the civil courts. The law was never intended to be taken into the hands of an individual; God knew the result would be utter chaos. You cannot have anarchy and preserve society. The intent of Mosaic law was to control sin—in this case, the sins of anger, violence, and revenge.

B. Explaining the Principle

Do you know what the statement "an eye for an eye, and a tooth for a tooth" (Matt. 5:38) means? Simply that the punishment must fit the crime—no less and no more. It was a restraint on the innate vengeance in the evil hearts of men. God wasn't saying to hurt the eye of someone who hurts your eye. Justice is never to go beyond its bounds. If only a tooth has been lost, then only a tooth should be taken. Yet the compensation for a lost tooth was usually money, not the other person's tooth. God was limiting the evil human heart, which always seeks to repay beyond the extent of the offence.

No one has ever murdered another person because that person murdered him! People who want to get even go way beyond the limits of the situation. A man will say, "You mess around with my girl friend, and I'll kill you." That's an overreaction. When the Lord said, "An eye for an eye, and a tooth for a tooth," He was putting boundaries on justice. That phrase does not refer to personal revenge.

Tit for Tat

Prescribing a punishment suitable for a crime is one of the oldest laws in the world. Known as the *lex talionis*, it is found even in the Code of Hammurabi, one of the earliest discovered law codes. Sometimes it's called tit for tat. The Code of Hammurabi says, "If a man has caused the loss of a gentleman's eye, his eye shall cause to be lost. If he shattered a gentleman's limb, one shall shatter his limb." This indicates a sense of justice in the human heart. However, that justice can often be perverted into vengeance.

It's good for a crime to be appropriately punished. God's law was meant to instill fear into the hearts of people and to help protect the righteous. Some people think we shouldn't allow ourselves to be encumbered by so many laws. But the stricter our laws are, the more protection the righteous will receive. The negative effects of a law hurt only those who deserve to be punished—evil people whose evil is out of control. There

9

are three things to point out about the law of just punishment:

1. It is a just law

    A punishment should fit the crime. Let me give you an illustration that does not go beyond justice: Judges 1:6-7*a* says, "Adoni-bezek fled; and they [some of the Israelites] pursued after him, and caught him, and cut off his thumbs and his great toes. And Adoni-bezek said, Threescore and ten kings, having their thumbs and their great toes cut off, gathered scraps of food under my table; as I have done, so God hath requited me." Adoni-bezek had cut off other people's thumbs and big toes, so he got his own cut off.

    In Iran, when a thief is caught, his hands are cut off. That has a tremendous effect on shoplifing! I'm not saying I want people's hands cut off, but if there aren't laws to instill fear in our hearts, we will pursue an evil path. Paul said, "Whatever a man soweth, that shall he also reap" (Gal. 6:7). Matthew 7:1 says, "Judge not, that ye be not judged." Luke 6:38*b* says, "With the same measure that ye measure it shall be measured to you again."

2. It is a merciful law

    "An eye for an eye, and a tooth for a tooth" is a merciful law because it limits vengeance. You may have heard stories like the following: A native from one tribe kills someone in another tribe. Consequently, the other tribe goes back to the first tribe and slaughters everyone they find. However, God's law says that only the person who committed the crime should be punished, and his punishment should be commensurate with the crime. That puts a lid on human vengeance. If a slave lost his tooth as the result of a brutal beating from his master, the slave could take his case to court and be set free. That law restrained evil masters from beating their slaves. Such a law never hurts those who are righteous.

3. It is a beneficial law

    The law Christ speaks of in Matthew 5:38 is designed to protect the weak from the strong. Our society has everything twisted: Today, it seems as if criminals have more rights than honest people! Our suffering society, overrun with crime and violence, would do well to reexamine Old Testament law. Once people deny God, their sense of justice is gone. The church must put this matter back into perspective again. It has to preach about God's just character, and it has to enact just, lawful discipline within itself. We need to preach about eternal punishment in hell so that the world will know there is right and wrong, with punishments and rewards. When the church became liberal and stopped preaching about the character of God, eternal punishment, the need for discipline, and sin, it stopped confronting society. It's possible that we have an effeminate generation that wants to abolish capital punishment, turn prisons into country clubs, and relax justice because the church hasn't been strong enough in its preaching of God's righteous standard. That's the legacy of theological liberalism.

To restrain evil is beneficient, merciful, and just. When evil is not punished, it will run rampant—and everyone will pay a price. Commentator Arthur Pink said, "Magistrates were never ordained of God for the purpose of reforming reprobates or pampering degenerates, but to be His instruments for preserving law and order, and that by being a 'terror to the evil'" (*An Exposition of the Sermon on the Mount* [Grand Rapids: Baker, 1974], p. 112). Romans 13:4b says that rulers are to "execute wrath upon him that doeth evil." Terror must be instilled in people's hearts to keep them from doing wrong. The law has been ignored because God's character, eternal punishment, and church discipline have been ignored.

Pink further said, "Conscience has become comatose: the requirements of justice are stifled: maudlin concepts now prevail. As eternal punishment was repudiated—either tacitly, or in many cases, openly—ecclesiastical punishments were shelved. The inevitable outcome has been the breakdown of discipline in the home and the creation of a 'public opinion,' which is mawkish and spineless. School-teachers are intimidated by foolish parents, so that the rising generation are more and more allowed to have their own way without fear of consequences. And if some judge has the courage of his convictions and sentences a brute . . . for maiming an old woman, there is an outcry raised against him" (p. 113). That is the legacy we have in our country.

Jesus upheld the Old Testament law stated in Matthew 5:38. He didn't attempt to change it. If God said that law was just, merciful, and beneficial, it has a reason for existing. In

Matthew 5:18-19 Christ says, "Till heaven and earth pass, one jot or one tittle shall in no way pass from the law, till all be fulfilled. Whosoever, therefore, shall break one of these least commandments, and shall teach men so, he shall be called the least in the kingdom of heaven." Our Lord came to fulfill the law, not destroy it (Matt. 5:17). In Matthew 5:38, He was not changing an Old Testament law; He was clarifying how God intended that law to be used.

C. Exercising the Principle

The law must be upheld; justice must rule. We must have a right sense of justice. But what should be our attitude toward those who break laws? Should we hate criminals? Are we to be vengeful? The Old Testament gives us insight.

1. Leviticus 19:18

This verse reads, "Thou shalt not avenge, nor bear any grudge against the children of thy people." Leviticus 24:20 says, "Eye for eye, tooth for tooth: as he hath caused a blemish in a man, so shall it be done to him." Moses wrote both of those verses. So you should never hold a grudge. If a crime is committed, then turn the matter over to the proper authorities—with a heart of forgiveness and love. That preserves society and exalts God. Jesus said, "Love your enemies, bless them that curse you, do good to them that hate you, and pray for them who despitefully use you, and persecute you" (Matt. 5:44).

I once had to stand at the door of my home to protect one of my children from a man with a knife. After that incident, I thought, *What would I have done if that man had killed my child?* Based on what Jesus taught, the proper response would be to have the man arrested. If he had been hungry or thirsty, I was to feed him. And if he needed Christ, I was to present the gospel to him. Most of all, I was to forgive him and love him at the same time that justice was done.

2. Proverbs 25:21

Here we read, "If thine enemy be hungry, give him bread to eat; and if he be thirsty, give him water to drink." We tend to think of an enemy as someone next door who has a yard full of weeds that might spread to our yard. But Proverbs 25:21 is talking about a serious enemy, like the man who threatened to maim my child with a knife. The

Old Testament says that if your enemy is hungry, give him bread to eat. But it also says that if he commits a crime, you must take him to court.

3. Proverbs 24:29

This verse says, "Say not, I will do so to him as he hath done to me." Don't be vengeful. When Christ hung on the cross, He knew that in time His disciples would be murdered. He knew that through the ages many would be martyred for their faith in Him. Yet He said of His enemies, "Father, forgive them" (Luke 23:34). Christ knew justice would take its course. He knew if His enemies died without repenting of their sins they would spend eternity in hell. Yet while He was on earth, He expressed forgiveness toward them.

If someone kills one of my children, I am to forgive Him in the love of Christ. I must feed him, but at the same time let the law take its course so that God's divine standard is upheld. I can't say, "I will do so to him as he hath done to me" (Prov. 24:29).

II. THE PERVERSION OF JEWISH TEACHING

A. The Prevailing Pattern

The Pharisees had perverted the principle "an eye for an eye, and a tooth for a tooth" into an excuse for personal vengeance. They said if someone knocks out your tooth, knock his out. They interpreted God's law as a mandate for vengeance, not a limit. Their emphasis was wrong, and they used God's law to justify the hatred in their hearts. In Matthew 5:38-42, Jesus in effect tells them, "You are not righteous. If you were, you wouldn't seek vengeance."

B. The Proper Perspective

How can we find the balance between upholding the law of God and having a forgiving heart? A person will not hold grudges or seek vengeance if he has died to self. When you have died to self, there is no reason to defend yourself. But if you fight for your rights, you prove that what is most important to you is yourself.

Jesus died to self: He abandoned Himself to the Father's will, and died on the cross. Paul also died to self: He said, "Whether we live, we live unto the Lord; and whether we die, we die unto the Lord; whether we live, therefore, or die, we are the Lord's" (Rom. 14:8). In 1 Corinthians 15:31, he says, "In Christ Jesus, our Lord, I die daily." If Paul had lived for himself, he would have gone through life defending himself against his critics. But he never did that. Selfishness is defensive, vengeful, and reactionary. If we want to have the attitude Christ asks us to have toward our enemies, we must die to our selfish nature. When you die to self, you will glorify God by upholding the law and not striking at others out of personal anger.

Dying to Self

We must understand what it means to die to self. When you are forgotten, neglected, or purposely set aside and you sting from the insult, but are happy at being counted worthy to suffer for Christ, that is dying to self. When your good is evil spoken of, your wishes are crossed, your advice disregarded, and your opinions ridiculed, yet you refuse to let anger rise in your heart but take it all in patient, loving silence, that is dying to self. When you lovingly and patiently bear any disorder, irregularity, annoyance, and you endure waste, folly, extravagance, and spiritual insensibility as Jesus did, that is dying to self. When you are content with any circumstance, food, offering, clothing, climate, society, solicitude, and interruption by the will of God, that is dying to self. When you never care to refer to yourself in conversation, record your own good works, seek after commendation from others, and are content with being unknown, that is dying to self. When you see your brother prosper and you can honestly rejoice with him in spirit without feeling envy or questioning God, even though you have greater needs or more desperate circumstances, that is dying to self. When you can receive correction and reproof from one of less stature than yourself and can humbly submit inwardly as well as outwardly without rebellion or resentment rising up in your heart, that is dying to self.

Ask yourself this question: Am I dead to self? You will be empty of self-upholding the law of God in an evil society and displaying a heart filled with forgiveness—when you learn what Jesus meant by this: "If any man will come after me, let him deny himself, and take up his cross, and follow me" (Matt. 16:24).

Focusing on the Facts

1. Describe the mind-set people in our society have regarding rights (see pp. 1-2).
2. What kind of people does our society make heroes of? What kind of people do they look down on (see p. 2)?
3. How did the Jewish leaders of Christ's time interpret the principle in Matthew 5:38 (see pp. 2-3)?
4. Explain what happens when people fight for their rights (see p. 3).
5. What happened to man's sense of justice when he fell into sin (see p. 3)?
6. Why did God establish law (1 Tim. 1:9-11; see p. 6)?
7. In what kind of situation does the law "an eye for an eye, and a tooth for a tooth" always appear in the Old Testament? What had the Pharisees done with that principle (pp. 6-7)?
8. Law is a ——————, and when —————— is enacted speedily and equitably, it has a great effect on —————— (see p. 7).
9. What happens if you give rights to a sinful man? What must parents do when their children exhibit bad behavior? Why (see p. 8)?
10. When God gave the principle, "an eye for an eye, and a tooth for a tooth," what was He saying (see p. 9)?
11. In what way is the law "an eye for an eye, and a tooth for a tooth" merciful? In what way is it beneficial (see pp. 10-11)?
12. What must be instilled in people's hearts to keep them from doing wrong (see p. 11)?
13. What should be our attitude toward those who break laws? Support your answer with Scripture (see pp. 12-13).
14. How did the Pharisees use the principle "an eye for an eye, and a tooth for a tooth"? Explain (see p. 13).
15. Give biblical examples of dying to self (see pp. 13-14).
16. Describe some of the characteristics of a person who has died to self (see p. 14).

Pondering the Principles

1. Have you sensed a retaliatory spirit within yourself lately? What caused you to have that feeling? When you have been hurt, it is important to make sure you don't respond in an ungodly way. What are some good ways for a Christian to deal with a vengeful spirit? Think of ways that other people upset you in the course of your day. How can you respond in a Christlike manner to those incidents? Whenever you encounter a situation that leaves you wanting vengeance, think about the way Christ would have

responded. Doing that will help you cultivate a more loving, forgiving heart.

2. People today still misinterpret the famous law, "an eye for an eye, and a tooth for a tooth" (Matt. 5:38). They believe it to be a biblical mandate for vengeance. How would you explain to someone what God really intended to do through that principle?

3. One way we can learn to respond properly to our enemies is to look at how people in the Bible responded to their enemies. Read the following verses: Genesis 37:18-28 with 50:19-21; John 18:1— 19:30; and Acts 7:54-60. What attitude did the people you read about display toward their enemies? Read Romans 12:17-21. What practical principles can you extract from that passage? (There are at least five.) Meditate on Romans 12:17-21, and let its message sink into your heart.

2
An Eye for an Eye—
Part 2

Outline

Introduction
A. The Confrontation of the Proud
    1. Announcing God's standard
    2. Denouncing man's standard
B. The Character of the Humble
    1. The human response of Paul
        a) The arrest
        b) The announcement
            (1) Ananias's reaction
            (2) Paul's response
        c) The apology
    2. The humble response of Christ

Review
I. The Principle of Mosaic Law
II. The Perversion of Jewish Teaching

Lesson
III. The Perspective of Jesus
    A. The instruction
        1. The principle of resisting evil
        2. The pattern for repaying evil
    B. The Illustrations
        1. The right to dignity
            a) Articulating the principle
            b) Applying the principle
        2. The right of security
            a) Articulating the principle
            b) Applying the principle
        3. The right of liberty
            a) Articulating the principle
            b) Applying the principle

4. The right of property
    a) Articulating the principle
    b Applying the principle

Conclusion

Introduction

A. The Confrontation of the Proud

Matthew 5:38-42 is a part of the great Sermon on the Mount (Matt. 5-7) preached by our Lord Jesus Christ. In the sermon, Christ told His listeners that they fell short of the standard for entrance into God's kingdom. He directed His sermon at the Jewish scribes and Pharisees because they had invented a system of religion that was unbiblical. It was based on human achievement, which consists of self-effort. The Jewish religious leaders believed that God would consider them righteous if they kept the low standards they had devised. But Jesus confronted the people who were a part of that religious system and attempted to knock the props out from under it. He knew the people He spoke to would not see their desperate need for a Savior until they saw the inadequacy of their religion. So in Matthew 5-7, the Lord showed the difference between divine truth and human wisdom—between the substandard religion of human achievement and God's religion of divine accomplishment. He wanted to destroy people's confidence in self-made Judaism and reassert God's standard.

1. Announcing God's standard

    The initial intent of the Sermon on the Mount is negative; Christ wanted to show people that they came short of God's standard. That is obvious from the contents of the Beatitudes. The first four verses talk about the need to be beggarly in spirit (Matt. 5:3), mournful over sin (v. 4), meek before God (v. 5), and seeking God's righteousness (v. 6). Christ wanted people to become desperate over their inadequacy. He said we don't have the resources to attain God's standard. Then, starting with Matthew 5:21, He shows the disparity between God's standard and the religious standards of His day. Before He could show that disparity, He needed to give them a Beatitude mentality. The Jewish religious leaders of that time were smug, proud, and egocentric. They thought God would usher

18

them into His kingdom. They were unrepentant, and had no sense of sinfulness or unworthiness. Thus, they had to come to the place where they would have a Beatitude heart.

Jesus endeavored to destroy the man-centered religion of His time. He began by telling people what God's standard was, and emphasizing that they hadn't attained it. In Matthew 5:21-48, He compares their system with God's truth. Several times, He began His comparison with these words: "You have heard it said . . . but I say unto you" (vv. 21-22, 27-28, 31-32, 33-34, 38-39, 43-44). He said, "You think it's enough not to kill, but God says don't even get angry (vv. 21-22). You think it's good if you don't commit adultery, but God says you shouldn't even think about it (vv. 27-28). You say it's OK to allow divorce if you do the proper paperwork, but God says don't divorce except in cases of adultery (vv. 31-32). You think it's enough to confirm your words with oaths, but you should always be truthful and not even need oaths (vv. 33-37). And if you think vengeance is proper, it's not. God says you shouldn't have a retaliatory spirit at all. You say, 'Love your neighbor and hate your enemy,' but God says, 'Love your enemy'" (vv. 43-44).

2. Denouncing man's standard

The Jewish religious system was substandard. It dealt with external behavior only—not sinful, internal attitudes such as anger, hatred, and lust or godly attitudes like truthfulness, love, and forgiveness.

The Sermon on the Mount is a sermon on sin. Christ preached it to show we are sinners. He wasn't preaching it only to those on the Galilean hillside; the message is for us too. There are people today who are proud of themselves because they haven't killed anyone, but they have anger and hate within them. Some of us are proud because we've never committed adultery, yet the thought of it has been in our minds. We are proud because we keep our word when we make an oath, but there are other times when we've lied. Some of us think we are fair to people, but we're really vengeful. We pride ourselves on our love for others, yet our enemies aren't within the purview of that love. Through the Sermon on the Mount, Christ wanted to destroy the confidence people had in their human religious systems and make them realize their need for a Savior. But He couldn't talk about their need until people saw the inadequacy of human achievement and began to search for a righteousness they could not attain on their own.

B. The Character of the Humble

Let's focus on one of the comparisons Christ made between God's standard and the Jewish religious standard: "Ye have heard that it hath been said, An eye for an eye, and a tooth for a tooth; but I say unto you that ye resist not evil, but whosoever shall smite thee on thy right cheek, turn on him the other also. And if any man will sue thee at the law, and take away thy coat, let him have thy cloak also. And whosoever shall compel thee to go a mile, go with him two. Give to him that asketh thee, and from him that would borrow of thee turn not thou away" (Matt. 5:38-42).

At first reading, it may sound like Jesus wants us to be sanctimonious doormats. We might think, "You've got to be kidding! Turn the other cheek? Give my coat to someone who sues me for my shirt? Go two miles when I need to go just one? Lend my possessions to anyone who asks to borrow them?" Our sinful nature retaliates against doing such things.

Getting Out of the Sand Trap of Vengeance

Some time ago a dear man who wanted to express his love for me gave me a set of golf clubs that he made. On each club was the fish symbol that Christians frequently identify themselves with. I thought, "This is terrific! I've got sanctified golf clubs; maybe I'll knock ten strokes off my game!" I went golfing, and when I teed off, I said, "All right, Lord, this is Your club. Do something with it!" I hit a long shot, but I hooked the ball a bit and it went into a man's backyard. Unfortunately, the man was out in his yard at the time.

I heard the man bellow, "Nice shot!" and then an epithet that I won't repeat. I walked over to where the yard was, hoping that the golf ball hadn't hit the man or broken his patio window. When I got there, I saw that the ball had simply hit a small hill in the corner of the yard, and rolled down from there. That part of the yard was just dirt, so I hadn't done any damage. I said, "Could you please give me my ball back?" The man said, "I play golf too, buddy," and put the ball in his pocket. My first thought was, "If he wants that golf ball, I'll just tee up and hit him eight more!"

As I left, I began to think how sad it is that there are people who go through life alienating others. How much nicer it would be for him to act graciously and extend his love to others and be loved in return. That experience is an example of a time when I had to override the natural instinct to seek vengeance.

Christ was dealing with the matter of vengeance in Matthew 5:38-42. That our hearts are prone to retaliation is evidence enough that no system of human religion can deal with our sinful nature. We need a Savior; we need a righteousness beyond our own. Let's look at more illustrations so we can better understand what Christ was saying.

1. The human response of Paul

   a) The arrest

      In Acts 23, the apostle Paul was tempted to assert himself in a way he shouldn't have. In Acts 22, the Jews had Paul arrested by Roman authorities in the city of Jerusalem (vv. 22-24). But the Romans didn't know why they wanted Paul in prison (v. 30). The Jews were upset at Paul because he kept preaching about Christ. It was disconcerting to them to have someone preaching all over Jerusalem that the person they had crucified was none other than their Messiah. Hence they had Paul incarcerated. However, the captain of the Roman army knew that Roman law said a prisoner could not be held without a charge. So he released Paul from his chains and brought him before the Jewish religious leaders, saying, "I can't imprison this man unless you have a charge against him."

   b) The announcement

      Beginning with Acts 23:1, we read that Paul was brought before the Sanhedrin. He was familiar with the Sanhedrin because he was once a member of it. Some of the members had been fellow students with him under Gamaliel, and others were fellow Pharisees and persecutors of the church. Verse 1 says, "Paul, earnestly beholding the council [i.e., looking intently into the eyes of the Jewish religious leaders], said, Men and brethren, I have lived in all good conscience before God until this day." He was saying, "I don't have anything to accuse myself of. I can

21

look you in the eye and say there is no charge that can be justly laid to my account. I'm innocent."

(1) Ananias's reaction

Ananias, the high priest, became infuriated when he heard Paul's words. (The Ananias in Acts 23 is not the same Ananias Paul met in Acts 9.) He was a vile man; he literally stole the tithes that belonged to the common order of priests to pad his own coffers. He was involved in immoral deeds and had assassinated people who were in his way. Ananias was a vile prostitution of everything representative of the priestly office. Verse 2 tells us about his response to Paul: "The high priest, Ananias, commanded them that stood by him to smite him on the mouth." Ananias used the Greek verb *tuptō*, which means "to give a violent blow with the fist." He said to one of his henchmen, "Punch that man in the mouth!" Ananias was a vile man in an evil system. Paul's rights had been violated; he had done nothing wrong.

(2) Paul's response

Acts 23:3 says, "Then said Paul unto him, God shall smite thee, thou whited wall; for sittest thou to judge me after the law, and commandest me to be smitten contrary to the law?" Paul responded in anger, which he shouldn't have done. The term "whited wall" was a reference to hypocrisy. Walls at that time were generally piles of bricks and mud—ugly, brown dirt. People covered walls with whitewash to make them look nicer. When you called a person a whited wall, as Jesus called the scribes and Pharisees in Matthew 23:27, you were saying, "You look good on the outside, but on the inside you're dirty." Paul responded from his flesh; it was the kind of response he would have given before he came to Christ. He was wrong to react the way he did. The people around Paul and Ananias were shocked at Paul's response. They said, "Revilest thou God's high priest?" (Acts 23:4). It's interesting that the people were more shocked with Paul's words than they were when Ananias had

Paul struck in the face. Was it all right for the high priest to have one of his henchmen strike a man in the mouth but not for the man to retaliate? That shows their double standard. I'm sure they knew this traditional saying by the rabbis: He who strikes the cheek of an Israelite strikes the glory of God.

c) The apology

In Acts 23:5 Paul says, "I knew not, brethren, that he was the high priest; for it is written, Thou shalt not speak evil of the ruler of thy people" (see Ex. 22:28). He admitted he was wrong and then condemned himself with the Scriptures. I like that. Paul apologized, even when it was true that Ananias was a white-washed wall. Paul knew God would bring judgment upon Ananias. Except for the grace of God unbeknown to us, Ananias is now in eternal hell. God did smite him. Yet we are not to respond in personal relationships the way Paul did to Ananias.

2. The humble response of Christ

In John 18 we see Christ in a similar situation to Paul's in Acts 23. He was also before a tribunal, Verses 22-23 say, "When he [Christ] had thus spoken, one of the officers who stood by struck Jesus with the palm of his hand, saying, Answerest thou the high priest so? Jesus answered him, If I have spoken evil, bear witness of the evil; but if well, why smitest thou me?" Christ was struck just as Paul was, yet He responded with a different spirit. He said, "If I've done evil and I deserve to be hit, let Me know. But if I've not done evil, why did you hit Me?" The Lord was forcing the man who hit Him to think of his deeds before he did them. He wasn't thinking about Himself. He said, "Make sure you have a reason for doing what you do, and make sure your actions are valid." He did not retaliate. First Peter 2:23 says that when Jesus was reviled, He "reviled not again." He never retaliated. Christ didn't sin, but Paul did.

How do you react to situations like that? Are you like Jesus? Do you say to your enemy, "You should think about your actions before you do them"? Let's look at Matthew 5:38-42 and find out how we should respond.

23

Review

I. THE PRINCIPLE OF MOSAIC LAW (see pp. 5-13)

This principle appears in Matthew 5:38: "Ye have heard that it hath been said, An eye for an eye, and a tooth for a tooth." Christ was referring to a traditional teaching of Judaism, which had originated from the Mosaic law. That principle is recorded in Exodus 21:24, Leviticus 24:20, and Deuteronomy 19:21. According to the contexts in which the phrase appears, it was a stipulation for law courts, not a mandate for vengeance in personal relationshps. That's why God brought about law courts and judges. The principle in Matthew 5:38 was known as the *lex talionis* in ancient times; it is the principle of exact retribution, which says that the punishment should never exceed the crime. God established that principle to make sure that justice was fair. "An eye for an eye, and a tooth for a tooth" is the foundational principle of all human justice. Punishment is not to be excessive, and someone who does wrong is to be punished by duly constituted authorities, not just anyone.

Human relationships and courts of law are two different things. For example, if a person commits a crime, we don't want the court to say, "We're so sorry about what you did. We want to be gracious and merciful, so we will forgive you. Just go out and remember that if you commit a crime again, we will forgive you again. We will even forgive you seventy times seven." If that happened, we'd have absolute chaos. We don't want the court to express mercy; its role is to serve justice and preserve society.

We also would not want a human relationship to function like a court. Suppose your wife does something that offends you. You wouldn't say, "All right; bend over. You offended me, so now I'll punish you." The law of just punishment belongs in the courts, not in the home. If your neighbor borrows something from you and breaks it, you don't go over to his house and say, "I'm going to break one of your possessions." Personal relationships are not to be handled that way. There must be a distinction between what is appropriate for law courts and what is appropriate for personal relationships. Courts are designed to punish wrongdoings fairly, and human relationships are to operate on the basis of love and forgiveness.

II. THE PERVERSION OF JEWISH TEACHING (see pp. 13-14)

The Jewish leaders Christ was speaking to in the Sermon on the Mount had taken the *lex talionis* out of the courts and applied it to their personal lives. They allowed vengeance to be a part of their relationships with others. But God had not intended that to happen.

Lesson

III. THE PERSPECTIVE OF JESUS

A. The Instruction

In Matthew 5:39 Jesus tells the scribes and Pharisees the attitude they should have toward their enemies: "I say unto you that ye resist not evil." That verse has been subject to misinterpretation by many people. They say, "If we are not to resist evil, then we are to be absolutely passive. We should let others walk all over us, hit us, abuse us, and steal all that we own. We must not be concerned about the sins of others. Evil is all around us, and it will take its course." But that's not what Christ was saying.

1. The principle of resisting evil

There are some passages in the Bible that talk about resisting evil. James 4:7 and 1 Peter 5:9 tell us to resist the devil. When you sense that Satan is attacking you, don't say, "Well, Satan, here you are again. Go ahead and do whatever you want." We are to resist evil. When Peter sins in Galatians 2:11-14, Paul doesn't say, "There goes Peter. Poor fellow, sin's got a hold on him." He said, "Peter you're not supposed to do that. Cut it out!" Paul withstood Peter to the face. First Corinthians 5 says that if you find someone in your congregation who is committing fornication, put him out of the church. According to 1 Timothy 5:19-20, if an elder is caught in sin, he is to be rebuked before the whole church. In Matthew 18 Jesus says that if a believer sins, you are to confront him. If he doesn't listen to you, take two or three others with you to rebuke him. If he still doesn't respond, tell the church about his sin. If at that point the sinning believer still refuses to repent, then put him out of the church.

We are to deal with our own sins and the sins of fellow believers. We are also to resist crime. Romans 13:1-2 says, "The powers that be are ordained of God. Whosoever, therefore, resisteth the power . . . shall receive to themselves judgment." God ordained governments to protect the good and punish the evil. If we don't uphold the government, we won't be upholding a God-given institution. We are to uphold the standards of the government. If we witness a crime, we are to call the police. Don't ignore crime, because the agents of government are ministers "of God to thee for good . . . [and] beareth not the sword in vain" (Rom. 13:4).

We resist evil in society by our laws, in churches by our purity, and in relationships by confrontation. In John 2 we see Jesus resisting evil when he makes a whip and cleanses the Temple (vv. 14-16). He does the same thing again in Mark 11:15-17. He didn't become a doormat to evil. God has given us a sense of self-preservation. If someone threatens to harm me or my family, it's normal for me to become protective. It's OK to protect yourself, your family, and your interests from harm. Proverbs 22:3 says, "A prudent man foreseeth the evil, and hideth himself." So when Christ said, "Resist not evil." He wasn't saying that we're to be doormats.

2. The pattern for repaying evil

What does Christ mean when he says, "Resist not evil" in Matthew 5:39? The word "resist" (Gk., *anthistēmi*) means "to set against," and the Greek term for "evil" is *to ponēros*, which refers to someone who wrongs you. Christ was saying not to set yourself against someone who wrongs you. Don't start a feud or seek vengeance. He wasn't saying we are to let evil overrun our lives, or that we can't protect ourselves from someone who violates our rights. Matthew 5:39 isn't a principle restricted to the Sermon on the Mount; it's found throughout Scripture.

Romans 12:17-20 says, "Recompense to no man evil for evil. Provide things honest in the sight of all men. If it be possible, as much as lieth in you, live peaceably with all men. Dearly beloved, avenge not yourselves but, rather, give place unto wrath; for it is written, Vengeance is mine; I will repay, saith the Lord. Therefore, if thine enemy hunger, feed him; if he thirst, give him drink; for in so doing thou shalt heap coals of fire on his head."

There's a story about an Irish lady whose husband was always drunk. She went to a pastor and said, "I've done all I can to correct my husband's life. I've even chased him around with a frying pan." The pastor said, "Have you thought about heaping coals of fire on his head?" She replied, "I've thought of some awful things, but not

26

that!" She missed the point. To heap coals of fire on someone's head is simply to turn back hate with love. You embarrass a person when you respond to his hate with love. The pastor was saying to overcome evil with good.

B. The Illustrations

Jesus illustrated what He said about loving your enemies by talking about four basic human rights: dignity, security, liberty, and property. It is interesting that the Constitution of the United States guarantees those things to us.

1. The right of dignity

In our society, I have the right to be honored as a human being. I should be treated with dignity, respect, and kindness. I am a person made in the image of God, and I should be dealt with as such. We hear people say things like, "I'm a human being. I won't allow you to mistreat me. I have my rights. I can't be demeaned or dishonored." That's right. Every person is made in the image of God and is entitled to dignity. But you're not always going to get it. Sometimes others will treat you like you're a worm. You might be mistreated in a gas station, a restaurant, or even by your own family. Sometimes someone close to you will do something that will cause you to say, "What did I do to deserve that? Doesn't he realize I'm made in the image of God? I have a right to dignity!" But let's look at what Jesus taught.

a) Articulating the principle

In Matthew 5:39 our Lord says, "Whosoever shall smite thee on thy right cheek, turn to him the other also." The Jews said that the most demeaning act was to slap someone in the face. To have a fight with someone was to treat him as an equal, but a slap was contemptuous. It was considered doubly demeaning if a man slapped you with the back of his hand. Epictetus, a one-time Roman slave of the first century A.D. who became a Stoic philosopher, said it is better to be thrashed to death than slapped on the cheek. Notice that Jesus said, "Whosoever shall smite thee on thy *right* cheek" (emphasis added). Since most people are right-handed, the only way the right cheek can be slapped is if it's done with the back of one's hand. So even if you are doubly demeaned and your dignity is taken away, you are not to retaliate. Christ wasn't saying to let others grind you to pulp. He was talking about having a nonretaliatory, forgiving, loving spirit. When you are dishonored and your dignity is tread upon, don't retaliate; let it happen again.

b) Applying the principle

Some people who misinterpret Matthew 5:39 say, "When Jesus was struck by the soldier in John 18:22, He didn't turn the other cheek." He actually did, but not in the sense some people would think. In verse 23 He tells the soldier, "If I have spoken evil, bear witness of the evil; but if well, why smitest thou me?" After that, He turned His cheek many times, for He was badly beaten. Isaiah 50:6 says, "I gave my back to the smiters, and my cheeks to them that plucked off the hair; I hid not my face from shame and spitting." Before Jesus was crucified, He was spat upon, a crown of thorns was put on His head, and He was mocked, beaten, and whipped. But He didn't retaliate against His enemies. Then when He was hanging on the cross and all His internal organs were being suffocated, He said, "Father, forgive them; for they know not what they do" (Luke 23:34).

When Jesus said "Resist not evil" (Matt. 5:39), He was saying, "When someone treats you in a disrespectful way, allow yourself to be slapped again before you would ever think to retaliate. Take as much disrespect as people will give you without thinking about vengeance." Don't worry about your dignity here on earth. Someday you'll be a son of God in the image of Jesus Christ. You'll stay that way forever, and the Lord will pour out all the goodness of His grace on you. Don't fight for your dignity now; you'll get it later. If you do fight for it, you'll disavow that you're a son of God and that you're related to Christ because you won't be acting in a way consistent with His ways.

2. The right of security

a) Articulating the principle

Nineteenth-century English minister C. H. Spurgeon said that we "are to be as the anvil when bad men are the hammers" (*Spurgeon's Expository Encyclopedia*, vol. 1

[Grand Rapids: Baker, 1977], p. 474). That's true. Sometimes people will take advantage of us. Matthew 5:40 says, "If any man will sue thee at the law, and take away thy coat, let him have they cloak also." You say, "Wait a minute! If someone tries to sue me, I'll get back at him." No. Jesus said, "Let him sue you, and then give to him." He wasn't saying to let just anyone sue you. If that were the case, unbelievers would sue us constantly and take everything we have. We'd be saying, "Do you want my house? Here, take it. How about my car?" Christ was talking about a lawsuit in which there is a justifiable reason to sue.

Notice that the person in Matthew 5:40 is being sued for his coat. The Greek word for "coat" in that verse refers to a tunic. In those days, a tunic was an undergarment, somewhat like a full-length shirt. Men didn't wear pants then as they do today; both men and women had long undergarments. A poor person might have only one. In Matthew 5:40 the phrase "at the law" indicates that the person being sued had been taken to court. Apparently there was justification for this lawsuit, and disputes are to be decided in court.

The person being tried in Matthew 5:40 doesn't have anything to pay except what he is wearing. Proverbially, Christ was referring to someone out to get your shirt. If someone sues you and gets your shirt, you are to show how sorry you are for the trouble you caused him and give him your coat as well. To any Jewish person, that would have been absolutely devastating. Their response to what Jesus said would have been, "But Exodus 22:26-27 says, when a tunic is given as pledge, it has to be returned by nightfall. How can anyone sleep at night without some kind of blanket? Everyone has a right to security. No one should be stripped naked and left to the elements."

b) Applying the principle

It's true that a person had to have something to keep himself warm, for it gets cold in Israel at night. A cloak was a man's last security; it kept him warm during the day and he would use it as a blanket at night. If it was taken as a pledge, it had to be returned at night. In Matthew 5:40 Jesus is saying, "If someone takes you to court and you have to give him your shirt, don't begrudge him. Don't retaliate or get angry. Show him you're sorry you caused him trouble. Show him you're so magnanimous that you're willing to give him your cloak, which is your last bit of security." If you do that, you will shock him. You will be showing him the love of Christ—the love spoken of in Matthew 5:44: "Love your enemies, bless them that curse you, do good to them that hate you, and pray for them who despitefully use you, and persecute you."

If someone has the nerve to sue you for something you did and take everything you've got, show him that you care for him by giving him more than he asks for. Some people can't imagine doing that. But if you do, you'll show that you are a son of the Father (Matt. 5:45).

Ludicrous Litigation

Don't be in a hurry to sue other people. In 1 Corinthians 6:1-8 Paul says not to sue fellow believers. A news reporter recently told me, "I met a radio and television minister who is without a doubt the most litigious man I've ever met. I've never met anyone who was so in a hurry to sue everyone for everything he could get!" What kind of a testimony for Christ is that? Don't be constantly fighting for your rights and suing other people. In 1 Corinthians 6:7-8 Paul says it's better to be defrauded than to take a brother of Christ to court. Be forgiving; show that you're a son of God. The situation in Matthew 5:40 assumes that the believer has been taken to court, not that he's there to sue someone else. There will be times when the court will have to make judgments about disputes. But we should not go around seeking to get everything we can out of other people.

3. The right of liberty

We have a right to freedom. God has made us independent. We all have our own brains, feet, hands, eyes, and ears. We have a great amount of freedom in where we go, what we do, and what we say. God has made each of us so unique that we're like snowflakes—no two people are alike.

a) Articulating the principle

Sometimes people will encroach on your freedom. There have been times in my life when I say to my wife, "Patricia, we have some time on our hands" and all of a sudden something will come up and I'll have to go somewhere. You may have experienced that too and said, "Do I have to give up my whole life for everyone else? I've got my rights! I'm entitled to some freedom." But in Matthew 5:41 Jesus says "Whosoever shall compel thee to go a mile, go with him two."

An Unexpected Call to Service

Many people think that the Pony Express was an American invention. Actually the idea came from the ancient Persians. They had a very sophisticated postal system. Their country was marked off into segments, and they had little way stations separated by one day's journey all over the country. At that time, the Persian Empire was very large. The men who delivered the mail would ride a horse from dawn until sunset, and when they reached the way station at the end of the day, there would be fresh horses and provisions waiting for them. Those men were called *aggareus*, or couriers. The Romans used that Persian term to refer to the same thing. In the Persian postal system, if the courier became sick or injured, he could conscript a citizen along the way and force him to finish the day's journey. So the *aggareus* became the courier who was conscripted.

When we see the Greek form of the word, *aggareuō*, in the New Testament, it refers to when a government official conscripted someone for public duty. When Jesus could no longer carry His cross to Golgotha to be crucified, the Romans conscripted a man named Simon of Cyrene to carry it (Matt. 27:32). He became an *aggareus*; the government compelled him to carry Christ's cross.

Wouldn't it be interesting if that could still be done today? Imagine yourself driving on the road, in a hurry to get to wherever you're going. Suddenly you see a police car behind you with flashing lights, and you pull over. The policeman comes to you and says, "I don't know what your plans are, but I have a little package that I want you to take to Sacramento today." You might say, "I can't go to Sacramento now; I've got other things to do!" In Persia, a citizen couldn't argue. People in the Roman Empire knew that they could be conscripted at any time, just as Simon of Cyrene was.

31

b) Applying the principle

It was common for Roman soldiers to get someone to carry their packs for them. However, there was a rule that they could never ask any one citizen to carry a pack for more than one mile. Sometimes a soldier would ask a Jew to carry his pack. The Jews hated the Roman soldiers and the idea of carrying the weapons of warfare that were used against their own people. But Jesus said, "If someone infringes on your liberty and asks you to go one mile, go with him two." You say, "That's hard to do." That's true, but that's the spirit of our Father in heaven. If God had gone only one mile with us, we would be in real trouble. But He carried our burden far beyond that.

Don't be concerned with your liberty, security, or dignity. God will give you the freedom of the sons of God. He will give you the security of His home in heaven forever, and He will give you the dignity of the image of Jesus Christ. Don't chase things here on earth that destroy the testimony God wants you to bear.

4. The right of property

Someone once said to me, "Everything I own is paid for." Wouldn't it be great to be able to say that? If someone needed something, you could give it to him without worrying that you are still paying for it. We are very possessive today. Suppose a friend of yours asks if he can borrow your car. You tell your wife, "So-and-so wants to borrow the car. What do you think?" Some of us would answer, "We just waxed the car. Your friend has kids; I can just see their muddy feet and sticky hands. That guy hits curbs all the time. If we loan the car to him, we'll have to have the wheels aligned again."

a) Articulating the principle

We are very possessive about our property. But Jesus says in Matthew 5:42, "Give to him that asketh thee, and from him that would borrow of thee turn not thou away."

b) Applying the principle

You say, "Surely there must be some qualifications to what Christ said in Matthew 5:42." Yes; He was talking about giving to those who have a real need.

You shouldn't help habitual beggars because that just encourages them to remain beggars. There are little children in Israel and other parts of the world who make a living begging because they've learned that they can play on the sympathy of tourists. But if someone has a need and asks you for something, give it to him. Don't say, "What for?" Just give from your heart. If you don't desire to help those in need, that's evidence that the religious system you're involved in isn't biblical.

Give to those who ask of you, and don't turn away those who want to borrow from you. That is the principle of self-sacrificing generosity. Deuteronomy 15:7-8 says, "If there be among you a poor man of one of thy brethren within any of thy gates in thy land which the Lord thy God giveth thee, thou shalt not harden thine heart, nor shut thine hand from thy poor brother; but thou shalt open thine hand wide unto him, and shalt surely lend him sufficient for his need, in that which he lacketh." Meet the needs of others. Don't buy off your conscience; be generous.

Conclusion

When Jesus taught that we are to be loving and forgiving (Matthew 5:38-42), He wasn't prohibiting justice. Rather, He was saying that justice belongs in the courts, and not in human relationships. If our rights are stolen—rights to dignity, security, liberty, or property—we are not to retaliate. We are to commit the situation to the Lord and act in love.

Nineteenth-century English philanthropist and evangelist George Mueller said this: "There was a day when I died, died to George Mueller and his opinions, preferences, tastes and will; died to the world, its approval of censure; died to the approval or blame of even my brethren and friends; and since then I have studied only to show myself approved unto God." That's the spirit we are to have. That's the spirit of Joseph, who generously forgave his brothers and showed his love for them (Gen. 50:19-21) even though they had sold him into slavery (37:18-28). David showed that spirit by sparing Saul's life twice, even though Saul wanted to kill him (1 Sam. 24, 26). Stephen showed forgiveness toward those who stoned him to death (Acts 7:60). Paul, after his conversion, wrote of love and forgiveness

(Romans 12:21; 1 Corinthians 4:12). And Jesus showed love and forgiveness when He said, "Father, forgive them" (Luke 23:34).

Focusing on the Facts

1. What did Christ tell His listeners in the Sermon on the Mount (see p. 18)?
2. What did Jesus do in Matthew 5:21-48? Explain (see p. 19).
3. What did those involved in Judaism need to see before they could see their need for a Savior (see pp. 19-20)?
4. What is one's first reaction likely to be when he reads Christ's words in Matthew 5:38-42? Why (see p. 20)?
5. What was Paul's reaction when Ananias had someone hit him (Acts 23:3)? Was it right for Paul to react that way? Explain (see pp. 21-23).
6. How did Christ respond when He was hit in John 18? Explain His response (vv. 22-23; see p. 23).
7. Explain the distinction between law courts and human relationships in regard to Matthew 5:38 (see p. 24).
8. In Matthew 5:39 Jesus says, "Resist not evil." Does that mean we are to be passive toward evil? Support your answer with Scripture (see pp. 25-26).
9. Why did God ordain governments (Rom. 13:1-2; see p. 25)?
10. Is it OK for us to defend ourselves from harm (Prov. 22:3; see p. 26)?
11. What does Christ mean when He says, "Resist not evil" in Matthew 5:39 (see p. 26)?
12. According to Romans 12:17-20, whom does vengeance belong to? What does it mean to "heap coals of fire" on the heads of our enemies (see pp. 26-27)?
13. What did slapping someone with the back of your hand mean in Christ's time? What did Christ say we are to do when that happens? What did He mean by that (see pp. 27-28)?
14. Why are you to give your cloak to someone who rightly sues you for your shirt? What will you show him by doing that (see pp. 29-30)?
15. Explain the cultural context of Christ's words, "Whosoever shall compel thee to go a mile, go with him two" (Matt. 5:41; see pp. 31-32)?
16. What qualification is there to Christ's words in Matthew 5:42? Should we help beggars? Explain (see pp. 32-33).
17. According to Deuteronomy 15:7-8, how are we to give (see p. 33)?
18. Summarize what Jesus is teaching in Matthew 5:38-42, and give some examples of people in the Bible who do that (see pp. 33-34).

Pondering the Principles

1. Read Matthew 5:21-37. Man, in his attempt to make himself feel good, will set standards for holiness that he is capable of meeting. The Judaistic system of religion in Christ's day had set its own standard for holiness. In contrast, Christ declared God's standard. A consistent pattern appears in Matthew 5:21-37: God's standard was always far above what the Jewish religious leaders had established. Because of our sinful nature, it's easy to slip in our commitment to keeping God's standards. With that in mind, answer the following questions: What negative effects would there be if you lowered your standards in these areas: commitment to family, personal purity, obedience to God, prayer time, study of God's Word, and good stewardship of finances? What are some ways you can keep yourself from lowering your standards in those areas?

2. Reread the shaded box on pages 20-21. Think of a recent situation where you felt like getting even with someone. What was your initial response to that person? How do you think Christ would have handled the situation? When you are in a situation where someone hurts you, it's helpful to think of how Christ would respond at that moment. Work on developing a habit of doing that.

3. Are there people at work, school, in your family, or in your neighborhood who are unkind to you? In what way have those people given you a hard time? How can you show love and forgiveness toward those people (i.e., heap coals of fire on their heads)? Write down your ideas, and when the opportunities arise, carry them out.

4. Christ did not seek to get even with those who hurt Him. Instead, He entrusted the matter to God. As an aid in remembering His example, memorize 1 Peter 2:23: "When they hurled their insults at him, he did not retaliate; when he suffered, he made no threats. Instead, he entrusted himself to him who judges justly" (NIV*).

*New International Version.

3
Love Your Enemies—
Part 1

Outline

Introduction
A. The Call to Follow the Lord's Standard
   1. In the New Testament
   2. In the Old Testament
B. The Compulsion to Follow the World's Standard
C. The Comparison of the Standards

Lesson
I. The Tradition of the Jewish Leaders
  A. Expressed
  B. Explained
  C. Examined
   1. The recipients of their selective love
     a) Jews in general
     b) Specific Jews
     c) Law-abiding Jews
   2. The rationale for their selective love
II. The Teaching of the Old Testament
  A. The Perverted Perspective
   1. Concerning the Canaanites
   2. Concerning the imprecatory psalms
  B. The Proper Perspective
   1. Concerning the Canaanites
   2. Concerning the imprecatory psalms
     a) Examining the psalmist's words
     b) Examining the psalmist's attitude

Introduction
There is a passage in Matthew 5 that deserves our greatest attention, for there is perhaps no other passage in all the New Testament that

sums up the heart and attitude of a Christian as well as this one. It talks about the most powerful testimony a Christian can have. In Matthew 5:44 Jesus says, "Love your enemies." That one statement by Christ sums up in the eyes of the world what Christians ought to be like. Historian Will Durant was asked how he would sum up the Christian ethic, and he said, "Basically, it's love your enemies. Without question Jesus set the highest ethic ever set in the history of man, but it's too bad no one lives up to it." Matthew 5:44 is the supreme facet of life: If love is the greatest thing, then loving your enemies is the greatest thing love can do. The summum bonum of kingdom living is found in the concept of loving our enemies.

A. The Call to Follow the Lord's Standard

1. In the New Testament

In all the Sermon on the Mount, there are two statements that sum up the standards of one who claims to be a member of the kingdom of heaven. One is in the middle of Matthew 5:47: "What do ye more than others?" Christ was saying, "What does your man-made system of religion have that makes it different from any other?" The other statement is in Matthew 6:8: "Be not ye, therefore, like unto them." Those statements sum up what Jesus was saying to His audience: "What do you do more than others? Don't be like everyone else." He was pointing out that His standards were not like any other standards. What He required of people was not what other people did. His standard was higher.

In His sermon, Christ indicted the pharisaical religious system as being substandard. He told the Jewish religious leaders, "What makes your system better than any other? What sets you apart? If you were in My kingdom, you wouldn't be doing what you are. The people in My kingdom have higher standards than you do." The Pharisees had the highest religious standard in Christ's time, but it wasn't high enough. God has a unique, holy standard for His kingdom. In Matthew 5:20 Jesus says, "Except your righteousness shall exceed the righteousness of the scribes and Pharisees, ye shall in no case enter into the kingdom of heaven." He was saying, "My standard is higher than the highest human standard: that of the scribes and Pharisees." Those religious leaders had many laws, ceremonies, and rituals—they were the most religious people of their time—yet God said, "You're no different than anyone else. My standard is that people do even more than you can do."

2. In the Old Testament

The highest human ethic always falls woefully short of God's standard. That concept isn't found only in the New Testament. God has always called His people to a higher standard. After He rescued the people of Israel from slavery in Egypt and made them His covenant people, He said, "I am the Lord your God. After the doings of the land of Egypt, wherein ye dwelt, shall ye not do; and after the doings of the land of Canaan, to which I bring you, shall ye not do; neither shall ye walk in their ordinances. ye shall do mine ordinances, and keep my statutes, to walk therein: I am the Lord your God" (Lev. 18:2-4). He was saying, "My standard is not like that of the Egyptians, whom you left, nor is it like that of the Canaanites, who live in the land you are going to."

Notice the phrase that appears at the beginning and end of what God said: "I am the Lord your God." The Lord was communicating to the Israelites, "Because I am the Lord your God, you should not act like anyone else. You should not live according to the standards of the Egyptians or the Canaanites." Since He was their covenant God and they were His chosen people, they were to be different from everyone else. They were to follow His commandments and not live by the standards of the people around them. But it's difficult to live according to a standard other than the one that engulfs us. It was hard for the Israelites, it was hard for those who lived in Christ's time, and it is hard for us today. However, that's what God asks.

B. The Compulsion to Follow the World's Standard

Unfortunately, through the centuries that followed God's command in Leviticus 18, the Israelites kept forgetting their uniqueness and continually fell into sin. The prophet Balaam said of them, "The people shall dwell alone, and shall not be reckoned among the nations" (Num. 23:9). They were supposed to dwell in isolation and not mingle with other nations. But in reality, they assimilated everything around them. Psalm 106:35 says the Israelites "mingled among the nations, and learned their works." What a sad commentary! The same thing can be said of the church. From the very beginning,

God has always called His people to a higher standard, yet for some reason they keep pulling it down.

In 1 Samuel 8:19-20 we read that the Israelites wanted a king: "We will have a king over us, that we also may be like all the nations." They wanted to be like the rest of the world. They even went so far as to say, "We will be as the nations, as the families of the countries, to serve [gods of] wood and stone" (Ezek. 20:32). So God sent prophets to remind Israel about her uniqueness. Jeremiah said, "Thus saith the Lord, Learn not the way of the nations" (10:2). Throughout Ezekiel, God says, "Defile not yourselves with the idols of Egypt" (20:7). Many prophets continuously pleaded with God's people. They said, "Be sure you maintain your unique standards. If you don't, you'll dishonor the Lord." The same plea applied to the people of Christ's time, and it still applies today. God wants His people to be different.

The standard Jesus presents in Matthew 5:44—loving your enemy—is not popular today. To most people, a statement like that sounds like lunacy. It doesn't make sense to them. That's because it's not an earthly standard; it's unique. In fact, it's a far greater ethic than you or I could ever keep on our own. It's beyond us to love our enemies. But citizens of the kingdom are to be distinct; you can't live the kingdom life unless you are infused with divine power.

C. The Comparison of the Standards

Throughout the Sermon on the Mount, Jesus tells the Pharisees, "Your system is substandard. Until you come to Me for power, you will never be able to live by My standards." The whole sermon draws a contrast between the best of men and the standard of God. Even the legalistic, religious Pharisees couldn't qualify to get into God's kingdom. They thought it was enough not to kill; Jesus said you are not to even be angry with your brother (Matt. 5:21-26). They thought it was enough to not commit adultery, but Christ said not to even think about it (5:27-30). They thought it was acceptable to get a divorce if all the legal paperwork was done, but the Lord said divorce was unbiblical except in cases of adultery (5:31-32). The Pharisees said it was enough to keep some vows; Jesus said you should be so truthful you don't even need to make vows (5:33-37). They thought it was right to take an eye for an eye and a tooth for a tooth, but our Lord said not to retaliate at all (5:38-42). In Matthew 6:5-15 He says their prayers are inadequate and tells them how to pray. He said their giving was wrong and told them how to give properly (6:1-4). In verses 19-34 He says, "You are concerned with material things. You should be seeking the kingdom of God." And in the passage we are studying now, He contrasts their love with the kind of love that should characterize citizens of the kingdom. Christ was telling the Pharisees that they weren't in His kingdom because they didn't meet God's standard.

God is calling us to be a separated people with convictions and standards that are not of the world. And nowhere is the distinction between man's life-style and the kingdom life-style made more clear—or more obscure—than in the life of a believer. Jesus confronted the Israelites because as religious as they were, they were still walking in the flesh. Their humanistic religious traditions fell woefully short of God's standard.

Lesson

This is what Christ says about the subject of love in Matthew 5:43-48: "Ye have heard that it hath been said, Thou shalt love thy neighbor, and hate thine enemy; but I say unto you, Love your enemies, bless them that curse you, do good to them that hate you, and pray for them who despitefully use you, and persecute you, that ye may be the sons of your Father, who is in heaven; for he maketh his sun to rise on the evil and on the good, and sendeth rain on the just and on the unjust. For if ye love them who love you, what reward have ye? Do not even the tax collectors the same? And if ye greet your brethren only, what do ye more than others? Do not even the heathen so? Be ye, therefore, perfect, even as your Father, who is in heaven, is perfect."

Jesus compares the Pharisees' standards with God's in five ways beginning in Matthew 5:21. In Matthew 5:43-48 Jesus presents the supreme contrast, because it's a statement about love, which is the greatest thing (1 Cor. 13:13), and the greatest way you can show love is to show it to your enemies.

The Key to Obeying the Ten Commandments

In Matthew 22 a lawyer comes to Jesus and asks Him, "Master, which is the great commandment in the law?" (v. 36). The Lord answered, "Thou shalt love the Lord, thy God, with all thy heart, and with all thy soul, and with all thy mind. This is the first and great commandment. And the second is like it, Thou shalt love

40

thy neighbor as thyself. On these two commandments hang all the law and the prophets" (vv. 37-40). Loving the Lord with all your heart, soul, and mind and loving your neighbor as yourself is like keeping all the laws of God. Paul says in Romans 13:8-10, "Owe no man any thing, but to love one another; for he that loveth another hath fulfilled the law. For this, Thou shalt not commit adultery, Thou shalt not kill, Thou shalt not steal, Thou shalt not bear false witness, Thou shalt not covet; and if there be any other commandment, it is briefly comprehended in this saying, namely, Thou shalt love thy neighbor as thyself. Love worketh no ill to its neighbor; therefore, love is the fulfilling of the law."

Paul and Jesus said love fulfills the whole law. So when our Lord speaks about love in Matthew 5, He touches on that which sums up the law. What Jesus said was a devastating blow to the Pharisees. In fact, it was so direct that it must have curdled their blood when He said they could be compared to the heathen (vv. 46-47). Their love was no better than that of tax collectors and pagans. The people in God's kingdom have a love that is beyond the best love the world can ever know. They don't just love their neighbors and hate their enemies; they even love their enemies. In saying that, Christ indicted the Pharisees and showed them their need for a Savior.

Each of the six contrasts that appear in Matthew 5 basically discuss three major points: the teaching of the Old Testament, the tradition of the Jews, and the truth from Christ. Let's look at the contrast in Matthew 5:43-48.

I. THE TRADITION OF THE JEWISH LEADERS

A. Expressed

In Matthew 5:43, Jesus says, "Ye have heard that it hath been said, Thou shalt love thy neighbor, and hate thine enemy." The phrase, "Ye have heard that it hath been said" indicates that what follows was a Jewish tradition that had been passed down from generation to generation. Christ wasn't talking about something from the Old Testament. Then He said, "This is your system; this is what you have been taught by the rabbis: Love your neighbor and hate your enemy." According to the Jewish religious leaders, once you figured out who your neighbors were, you could hate everyone who wasn't your neighbor. Whether you loved or hated someone depended on your definition of a neighbor. If you said your neighbors are your wife and three best friends, you could hate the world.

B. Explained

The phrase "Thou shalt love thy neighbor" sounds pious. You say, "How did the Pharisees come up with that?" It's in Leviticus 19:18. Whenever the Jewish religious leaders wanted to make up a rule, they made sure that some apsect of it was supported by the Old Testament. That way, their rule was assured of being somewhat right, just as a clock that is right twice a day. Leviticus 19:18 says, "Thou shalt not avenge, nor bear any grudge against the children of thy people, but thou shalt love thy neighbor as theyself."

Notice there was something missing in the rabbinical teaching Christ mentioned in Matthew 5:43. The Pharisees taught, "Thou shalt love thy neighbor, and hate thine enemy," but Leviticus 19:18 says, "Thou shalt love thy neighbor *as thyself*" (emphasis added). That was a convenient omission. The Jewish religious leaders lived in a state of such unbelievable pride that rather than have to treat others equal to themselves, they dropped the phrase "as thyself." The person who came to Christ in Mark 12:33 and the lawyer in Luke 10:27 added "as thyself," but it may have been that he wanted to be accurate because he was talking to Christ. Otherwise, the norm was, "Thou shalt love thy neighbor." They didn't want to love anyone else like they loved themselves; they were too proud of themselves to love anyone else equally.

How Much Do I Love Others?

Have you ever thought about what it means to love someone as you love yourself? If you were to just love someone and not have to love him as much as you do yourself, you could love him at a distance. You wouldn't have to treat him as well as you do yourself. You could show him one-half, one-third, or one-tenth of the love you show yourself. It would be so convenient to drop the little phrase "as thyself" in Leviticus 19:18 and say, "Love your neighbor," period. But the Lord wanted to drive His point right to the heart of our being: Love your neighbor as much as you love yourself.

How much do you love yourself? Everyone loves himself. Whose teeth did you brush this morning? Whose hair did you comb?

Whose wardrobe is in your closet? Whose money is in your savings account? You are concerned about yourself and take care of your needs. To love someone is to serve the needs of that person. You meet your needs; you have an unfeigned, unhypocritical, total love for yourself. There aren't some days when you fall out of love with yourself; you are always watching out for yourself. That love is genuine, habitual, and permanent. When you have an interest, you fulfill it. When you have a need, you meet it. When you want something or have a desire, you hope you will get it. You want to see your ambitions come to fruition. That's the way life is. You're very concerned about your own welfare, comfort, safety, interests, and health. You're concerned about physical, spiritual, temporal, and eternal things. You seek pleasure, and desire things for yourself.

The way you love yourself is the way you are to love everyone else—including your enemies! You are to have a consuming, unfeigned, fervent, habitual, permanent love for others that considers their interests, needs, wants, hopes, ambitions, welfare, safety, and comfort. You should be anxious to help fulfill another person's needs and wants.

How do you measure up? The last time you had a choice between doing what you wanted or sacrificing your wishes so someone else could do what he wanted, which way did you go? Whom do you really care about? God's standard is very high. Humanly speaking, to love your neighbor as yourself is impossible because we are so absorbed with ourselves. For example, look at your income. After taxes, you might use about 90 percent of your income on yourself or your family, and maybe give the Lord a percentage too. Compare how much you spend on yourself with how much you spend on the people who live on your street. You probably spend very little on them. But a comparison like that is meaningless to us because we don't think in terms of loving our neighbor as much as ourselves. To do that is very difficult, yet that's the way we're to love others.

C. Examined

1. The recipients of their selective love

    a) Jews in general

    The rabbinical teaching Christ discusses in Matthew 5:43 said, "Thou shalt love thy neighbor, *and hate thine enemy*" (emphasis added). Where did that last phrase come from? Nowhere does the Bible command us to hate our enemies. Apparently that concept was made up by the Jewish religious leaders. It was the logical extension of their perverted thinking. They said, "We have to love our neighbor. Now, let's determine who our neighbors are. Only Jews qualify, since Gentiles aren't neighbors." But they decided there were some Jews who didn't qualify either."

b) Specific Jews

We read about Jews who didn't qualify as neighbors in Matthew 9:9-10: "Jesus . . . saw a man, named Matthew, sitting at the tax office; and he saith unto him, Follow me. And he arose, and followed him. And it came to pass, as Jesus sat eating in the house, behold, many tax collectors and sinners came and sat down with him and his disciples." Jewish tax collectors were looked upon as traitors and extortionists. They were despised because they had sold themselves out to Rome for money. The sinners in Matthew 9:10 were probably criminals and prostitutes. Verse 11 says, "And when the Pharisees saw it, they said unto his disciples, Why eateth your Master with tax collectors and sinners?" So only Jews were considered neighbors, with the exception of Jewish tax collectors and sinners. In fact, one woman caught in the act of adultery is almost stoned in John 8:3-11.

c) Law-abiding Jews

The definition neighbor was narrowed even further by the Jewish religious leaders in John 7:49. There they said, "This people, who knoweth not the law, are cursed." They were referring to the many uneducated people who had no commitment to pharisaic tradition. The Pharisees eliminated from their circle of neighbors tax collectors, sinners, and anyone not committed to the law the way they were. The only neighbors they had were those within their own group! If you were one of them, you were loved, but if you were outside their group you were a hated enemy. Their motto was, "Us four, no more, bar the door!" They were committed to themselves and no one else.

2. The rationale for their selective love

The Pharisees fed their proud, evil hearts by concluding that anyone who wasn't a neighbor was to be hated. They said, "The Old Testament teaches we are to love our neighbor. Therefore, someone who isn't a neighbor is *not* to be loved." Since the opposite of love is hate, they concluded loving your neighbor means hate your enemy. That's what is known as a *non-sequitur*, an argument that doesn't follow through logically. But that's the way the Pharisees reasoned, because they had perverted hearts. Their prejudice found a way to hate people.

If the Pharisees had gone past Leviticus 19:18 and read on to verse 34, they would have seen this: "The stranger who dwelleth with you shall be unto you as one born among you, and thou shalt love him as thyself." They were to love those who weren't Jews as they loved themselves. Exodus 12:49 says, "One law shall be to him that is home-born and unto the stranger that sojourneth among you." There aren't different laws for different people. Your love for others is to be broad, just as the commandment of God is broad (Ps. 119:96).

The Pharisees weren't the only people who were selective about who they loved. All three sects of Judaism at that time—the Pharisees, the Sadducees, and the Essenes— were like that. The Essenes were like a hippie cult and lived in a community now known as *Qumran* on the edge of the Dead Sea. That's where the Dead Sea Scrolls were found. The Essenes lived apart from society and had a primitive life-style. They occupied themselves with making copies of Scripture and lived an austere, antisocial life. Among their writings were found these statements, which show they had the same attitude as the Pharisees toward outsiders: "Love all that God has chosen and hate all that He has rejected. Love all the sons of light, each according to his lot in God's community and hate all the sons of darkness, each according to his guilt in God's vengeance. The Levites curse all the sons of Belial." To them, the sons of Belial were those who weren't Essenes. They cursed anyone who wasn't a part of their group, just as the Pharisees did.

The love of the Jewish religious leaders was narrow and ugly. They thought they had license to hate anyone who didn't fit their definition of *neighbor*. If you don't think they were filled with hatred, observe their interactions with Christ in the New Testament. One of the evasive maxims of the Pharisees discovered by archaeologists was this: "If a Jew sees a Gentile fallen into the sea, let him by no means lift him out thence for it is written, 'Thou shalt not rise up against the blood of thy neighbor, but this man is not thy neighbor." If a Jew saw a Gentile drowning, he was to let him drown because Gentiles were not considered neighbors. With such an outlook, it's little wonder that the Romans charged the Jews with hatred of the human race.

It's possible to figure out how the Pharisees twisted Leviticus 19:18 to fit their own prejudices. Nowhere in the Old Testament does it say to hate your enemy, but there are some things in the Old Testament that can appear to support that principle. We're going to look now at where they got the idea to hate their enemies. After that, we'll clear up the misconceptions by looking at the truth of Christ.

II. THE TEACHING OF THE OLD TESTAMENT

A. The Perverted Perspective

1. Concerning the Canaanites

   The Pharisees wanted to justify their hatred so it wouldn't encroach on their self-righteousness. They had to invent some excuse for allowing hatred to be in their religious system. One excuse they found for hating their enemies was God's extermination of the Canaanites in the Old Testament (Josh. 3:10). At the time when God brought the Israelites to the land of promise, it was inhabited by the Canaanites, who were one of the most vile, wretched people on earth. In fact, archaeology has shown that there may not have been a race worse than they were. They sacrificed people to their gods, believed in blood-letting, massacred babies, and participated in horrible orgies. God wanted them to be wiped out. He also told Israel to wipe out the Amalekites (Deut. 25:19). Not only were they to be wiped off the face of the earth but the memory of them as well. God's command to remove evil groups of people from the Promised Land could have easily been interpreted to mean we're to hate our enemies. But how could the God who said, "Love your enemies," be the same one who said, "Wipe out the nations that are in the land before you?" That seems confusing.

46

2. Concerning the imprecatory psalms

The Pharisees probably also used the imprecatory psalms, where David praised God for His judgment on his enemies, as an excuse. People often say, "How can the Bible say we are to love our enemies when at the same time David asks God to punish his enemies and do away with them? How could David pray that way for his enemies when he's supposed to love them?" There's no doubt the Pharisees used the imprecatory psalms to justify their hatred toward certain people.

Psalm 69 is a good illustration of an imprecatory psalm. There, David calls judgment upon those who are evil. Notice the stirring maledictions he gives beginning with verse 22: "Let their table become a snare before them; and that which should have been for their welfare, let it become a trap. Let their eyes be darkened, that they see not; and make their loins continually to shake. Pour out thine indignation upon them, and let thy wrathful anger take hold of them. Let their habitation be desolate, and let none dwell in their tents. For they persecute him whom thou hast smitten, and they talk to the grief of those whom thou hast wounded. Add iniquity unto their iniquity, and let them not come into thy righteousness. Let them be blotted out of the book of the living, and not be written with the righteous" (vv. 22-28). David was saying, "God, give them both barrels; don't spare anything!"

The Pharisees used the Old Testament to justify their personal vendettas. However, they missed the point of the command to destroy the Canaanites and the words in the imprecatory psalms; neither have anything to do with personal relationships. Just as we learned in our study of the principle "an eye for an eye, and a tooth for a tooth" (Matt. 5:38), there are some things God intended to be used in the context of judicial matters and not personal relationships. The Jewish religious leaders misinterpreted the judicial code of Matthew 5:38 and applied it to their way of living. Likewise, they took the judicial acts of a holy God who intended to preserve a righteous people, and used them as justification for their hatred of certain people.

B. The Proper Perspective
1. Concerning the Canaanites

The Canaanites were a vile people. So nauseating and corrupt were their abominations that the Bible says, "The land itself vomiteth out her inhabitants" (Lev. 18:25). They were wretched people. When a person who has cancer goes to a doctor and the doctor removes the cancer, we don't say that the doctor is a cruel, unloving, uncaring person. Rather, we thank him for removing the cancer. When God wanted to get rid of the Canaanites, He was not being evil; He was doing society a favor by removing a vile people who were a cancer and would do nothing but pollute the land. That was a judicial act on God's part; it did not give license to a Jew to despise or hate a Canaanite. Just because God enacted judgment on the Canaanites doesn't mean He didn't love them with the same love He shows us. I love my children even when I punish them. The punishment results from their evil, but it doesn't deny my love for them.

Leviticus 18:26-30 says that if the Israelites had followed the customs of the Canaanites, they would have faced a similar fate. God wanted to preserve a righteous seed from whom would come a righteous Messiah to redeem the world. The preservation of Israel was of great concern to God. He wanted to have a witness in the world, and He was removing a cancer from human society. We have enough sense today, at least in some places in the world, to set apart individuals who are cancerous to society—those who kill, maim, and steal. God was doing the same when He judged the Canaanites; He was setting aside those who were evil for the good of society.

German theologian Dietrich Bonhoeffer wrote, "The wars of Israel were the only 'holy wars' in history, for they were the wars of God against the world of idols. It is not this enmity which Jesus condemns, for then he would have condemned the whole history of God's dealings with his people. On the contrary, he affirms the old covenant" (*The Cost of Discipleship* [New York: Macmillan, 1963], p. 163).

2. Concerning the imprecatory psalms

    a) Examining the psalmist's words

    In the example we looked at from Psalm 69, reading verse 9 helps to explain what David said in verses 22-28: "Zeal of thine house hath eaten me up." Why was David so upset and praying for judgment upon those who were evil? Because of what they had done to him? No, because of what they had done to the Lord. He wasn't showing hatred on a personal level.

The Balance Between Judicial and Personal Matters

One of David's greatest enemies was his own son Absalom. He prayed that God would judge his son (Ps. 3:7), and yet he cried from the deepest part of his heart, "O my son Absalom, my son, my son Absalom!" when he was killed (2 Sam. 18:33). That he prayed for judgment to glorify God and preserve His people doesn't mean he didn't love his son. We love the lost, yet we pray that their sin would stop and that God would be vindicated. Our hearts ache for those without Christ, yet we pray that Jesus would set up His kingdom and put the unrighteous aside. In the apostle John's vision in the book of Revelation, he ate a scroll that was both sweet and bitter (10:9-10). It was sweet to see Christ reigning, but it was bitter to see what would happen to the lost. There was a tension between his love for God and his love for unbelievers.

David prayed for judgment on the evil because, in his words, "Zeal of thine house hath eaten me up; and the reproaches of those who reproached thee are fallen upon me" (Ps. 69:9). He wasn't defending himself; he was defending God. It's one thing to defend the glory and honor of God; it's something else to hate people personally. The judgments and curses in the Old Testament were always judicial, not personal. My attitude toward anyone—even my worst enemy—is to be forgiving and loving, while at the same time I pray, "God, don't let Your enemies continue to dishonor Your name; take the glory that belongs to You." I am to love my enemy and pray for him to become saved. I should also pray that God will judge unbelievers so that He can bring Christ to be the rightful ruler of this world and set righteousness in its proper place again.

God punished Adam, but He loved him. He loved Cain, but He punished him. He loved everyone in the world at the time of Noah but drowned them in the flood. He loved Sodom and Gomorrah, but burned them to ashes. God loved the nation of Israel, but set them aside for a time. He loved His only begotten Son but let Him bear the sin of the world and die. And God loves the world today, but He promises that it's going to be burned up someday (2 Pet. 3:10-12). God loves you, but you'll spend eternity in hell if you don't know His Son.

The scribes and Pharisees never made any distinction in the

tension between judicial punishment and personal hatred. Their evil, perverse hearts took passages about judgment and used them as justification to hate people. That was wrong.

b) Examining the psalmist's attitude

In Psalm 139 David says, "Surely, thou wilt slay the wicked, O God; depart from me therefore, ye bloody men. For they speak against thee wickedly, and thine enemies take thy name in vain. Do not I hate them O Lord, that hate thee? And am I not grieved with those who rise up against thee? I hate them with perfect hatred; I count them mine enemies" (vv. 19-22). Notice that David expressed hatred. However, his was "perfect hatred" (v. 22). It's not right to be angry, but there is such a thing as righteous indignation. We are not to be angry when someone offends us, but we can express righteous indignation when someone dishonors God. Would it have been right for Jesus to say to an enemy, "Don't talk to Me that way," and punch him in the face? No; but it was right for Him to defend the holiness and honor of God with a whip (John 2:15-17).

There is a difference between human anger and holy wrath, between personal hatred and perfect hatred. David was expressing perfect hatred. He was saying, "I hate those who do evil, but not because they hate me. I'll forgive them and love them anyway. But I hate what they do to the Lord's honorable name." He says in Psalm 139:21-22, "Am not I grieved with those who rise up against thee? I hate them with perfect hatred." Then he says in verses 23-24, "Search me, O God, and know my heart; try me, and know my thoughts; and see if there be any wicked way in me." He was saying, "Check out my heart, Lord, and You'll see that my hatred is a perfect hatred. I'm not angry at a personal enemy of mine. Examine my heart, and see if that isn't true."

Perfect hatred is not personal. The thing that distinguishes Christians from everyone else in the world is our capacity to personally love our enemies. Yes, we pray for God's glory to be vindicated and for an end to the unrighteous who curse His name. We know that someday God will come in flaming vengeance. We know that the same Jesus who said, "Love your enemies" pronounces woes and doom on the Pharisees in Matthew 23. Somday, God will act in judgment. In defense of Him, we will uphold His holy name. But in our personal relationships, we are to be characterized by a love for our enemies. That makes us different from those who are in the world.

People in the world love their friends; they are fairly good at that. They also show love toward their families. They sometimes even show compassion and sympathy to those who don't have much. But they don't love their enemies. The people of the world may not kill, but they get angry. Some of them don't commit adultery, but they do in their hearts. They have different legal reasons for allowing divorces when they shouldn't have divorces. Unbelievers keep their word sometimes, but they should always do that. They will retaliate; they don't always forgive and forget. Unbelievers may love others, but they don't love their enemies.

In Matthew 5:43-44 Jesus in effect says, "I don't want you to love as the world does. You are to love everyone, including your enemies." In verse 47 He tells those who don't love their enemies, "What do ye more than others? What makes you different?" You won't be different if you just sprinkle a little Christian activity on your human life. You won't be different if you just commit a small part of yourself to Christ. A person who belongs to the Lord's kingdom loves his enemies. That's a high standard. John Stott said, "To 'love' them is ardently to desire that they will repent and believe, and so be saved" (*Christian Counter-Culture: The Message of the Sermon on the Mount* [Downer's Grove, Ill.: InterVarsity, 1979], p. 117). If you love your enemies enough, they might respond to the Christ who lives in you. The Lord is made visible in our lives through such love.

Focusing on the Facts

1. What two statements in the Sermon on the Mount sum up the standards of a Christian? What was Jesus communicating to His listeners in those statements (see p. 37)?
2. What did Jesus say about the pharisaical religious system? Explain (see pp. 37-38).
3. Explain the significane of the phrase "I am the Lord your God" in Leviticus 18:2-4 (see p. 38).
4. Did the Israelites stay committed to God's standard in the

centuries after Leviticus 18? Why did they do what they did? Support your answer with Scripture (see p. 38).

5. What is the thrust of the Sermon on the Mount (see pp. 39-40)?
6. Nowhere is the ——————— between man's life-style and the kingdom life-style made more clear—or more obscure—than in the ——————— of a ——————— (see p. 40).
7. What is the greatest way you can show love (see p. 40)?
8. How does biblical love relate to the Ten Commandments? Support your answer with Scripture (see pp. 40-41).
9. Why did the Pharisees drop off the phrase "as thyself" (Lev. 19:18) in their teaching about loving your neighbors (see p. 42)?
10. Describe the kind of love you should have for others (see pp. 42-43).
11. Toward whom did the Jewish religious leaders show love? Whom did they reject (see pp. 43-44)?
12. Why did the Pharisees conclude that they were to hate their enemies? What does Scripture say about how strangers are to be treated? (see pp. 45-46).
13. How did the Pharisees use Scripture to justify their hatred for their enemies (see pp. 46-47)?
14. What was wrong with the way the Pharisees had used the old Testament to justify their hatred toward enemies (see p. 47)?
15. God's judgment upon the Canaanites cannot be considered a license for us to hate our enemies. Why did God judge the Canaanites (see pp. 47-48)?
16. Was David showing personal hatred toward evil people in Psalm 69? Explain (see pp. 48-49).
17. Give some examples in which the tension between judicial matters and personal relationships exist (see pp. 49-50).
18. What kind of hatred did David have in Psalm 139:19-22? Explain (see p. 50).
19. The thing that distinguishes us as Christians from everyone else in the world is the ——————— to personally ——————— our ——————— (see p. 50).
20. How is the Lord made visible through our lives (see p. 51)?

Pondering the Principles

1. In the Sermon on the Mount, Jesus asks His audience, "What sets you apart from everyone else?" Think about the people you interact with from day to day, such as your relatives, neighbors, friends, coworkers, or fellow students. What sets you apart from those people? Spend some time thinking about what your testimony to the world is now, and what it could be. Challenge

yourself and set some new goals that will help your testimony shine brighter for Christ.

2. You are to love others as much as you love yourself. Although that's difficult to do, we should make a conscious effort to think about the interests, needs, welfare, safety, and comfort of others. Write a list of the names of some of the people you know. Each week choose two or three people from that list, and think of a way you can express your love for them in fulfilling their needs or wants. Making that activity a regular part of your life will help you to develop a greater concern for others.

3. A true test of your Christianity is your willingness to love those who are your enemies. Get together with a friend or your family and discuss the following: What are some reasons that God wants us to love our enemies as well as our neighbors? Do you have a genuine love for your enemies? Think of specific people you don't get along with. What are some good ways to show love toward them?

4
Love Your Enemies—
Part 2

Outline

Introduction
A. Presenting the King
B. Presenting the King's Standards

Review
I. The Tradition of the Jewish Leaders
II. The Teaching of the Old Testament
   A. The Perverted Perspective
   B. The Proper Perspective
     1. Concerning the Canaanites
     2. Concerning the imprecatory psalms
       a) Examining the psalmist's words
       b) Examining the psalmist's attitude

Lesson
     3. Concerning a friend's possessions
     4. Concerning an enemy's possessions
     5. Concerning an enemy's problems
     6. Concerning retaliation
       a) Psalm 7:3-5
       b) Psalm 35:12-16
       c) Proverbs 17:5
       d) Proverbs 24:29
     7. Concerning peaceful relations with enemies
       a) Abram and Lot
         (1) The situation
         (2) The response
       b) David and Saul
         (1) The situation
         (2) The response

Introduction

Let's read verses 43-48 of Matthew chapter 5: "Ye have heard that it hath been said, Thou shalt love thy neighbor, and hate thine enemy; but I say unto you, Love your enemies, bless them that curse you, do good to them that hate you, and pray for them who despitefully use you, and persecute you, that ye may be the sons of your Father, who is in heaven; for he maketh his sun to rise on the evil and on the good, and sendeth rain on the just and on the unjust. For if ye love them who love you, what reward have ye? Do not even the tax collectors the same? And if ye greet your brethren only, what do ye more than others? Do not even the heathen so? Be ye, therefore, perfect, even as your Father, who is in heaven, is perfect."

A. Presenting the King

In his gospel, Matthew presents Jesus Christ as King. He begins by discussing His royal birth from a royal lineage. He writes about the adoration of the Persian kingmakers known as the *magi*, who recognized Jesus as King. In Matthew 3, he speaks of Jesus' baptism, during which God approved of Him as the anointed one by saying, "This is my beloved Son, in whom I am well pleased" (v. 17). Matthew then talks about Christ's victory over Satan, the reigning monarch of the earth. Satan tempted Christ three times, and each time he was defeated. Christ's kingliness is seen in His power over the physical world. He raised the dead, gave sight to the blind, hearing to the deaf, voices to the speechless and enabled the lame to walk. Matthew wrote all those things to present the majesty of Christ.

B. Presenting the King's Standards

In chapters 5, 6, and 7, Matthew presents the standards of the Lord's kingdom. He knew people would say, "If Christ is the King, what are the rules of His kingdom? What is the manifesto of the Monarch?" The incomparable Sermon on the Mount presents those standards. The key thing about the standards of the Lord's kingdom is that they are not the same as those of the world. In fact, Jesus contrasted them with the religious system of His day. He showed how inferior Judaism was to the standards of His kingdom. The Jewish people had taken God's divine standards and lowered them to their own level. Then when they kept their substandard rules, they identified themselves as righteous—with a righteousness they themselves had invented.

Jesus came to lift up the standard. He didn't change the Old Testament rules or put them aside, He reaffirmed them. He does that through a series of six contrasts in Matthew 5. Beginning with verse 21, He contrasts the Jewish religious leaders' view of murder with His. Then He contrasts their views of adultery, divorce, swearing, retaliation, and love with His. When Christ talked about their view of love, He reached an apex, for the apostle Paul said love is the greatest thing (1 Cor. 13:13). Jesus saved His view on love for last as His ultimate contrast; it was the epitome of the disparity between the standards of His kingdom and those of the people of His time. Matthew 5:43-44 says, "Ye have heard that it hath been said [a reference to rabbinical teaching], Thou shalt love thy neighbor, and hate thine enemy; but I say unto you, Love your enemies." That's the disparity that existed between the low, substandard religious ethic and God's ethic.

Review

In each of the six contrasts in Matthew 5, there are three features: the tradition of the Jews, the teaching of the Old Testament, and the truth of Christ.

I. THE TRADITION OF THE JEWISH LEADERS (see pp. 41-46)

As Christ says in Matthew 5:43, the Jewish religious leaders taught, "Thou shalt love thy neighbor." That sounds good, and it is taught in the Old Testament (Lev. 19:18). However, any system that wants to infiltrate or substitute the truth will have a portion of truth in it, and therein lies the deceit. Ephesians 4:14 says, "Be no more children, tossed to and fro, and carried about with every wind of doctrine." Whenever Satan encroaches upon the truth, he invariably maintains a portion of it to make whatever he is propagating look right.

The Jewish rabbinical teaching said, "Thou shalt love thy

neighbor." However, there are two problems with that: Something was left out, and something else was added. The phrase "as thyself" was left off from Leviticus 19:18, and in its place was added "and hate thine enemy." The Jewish religious leaders did not want to love others as much as themselves because of their pride, and they wanted to justify their hatred toward anyone who wasn't a part of their group. They conveniently dropped a phrase, added another to a portion of Leviticus 19:18, and ended up perverting God's standard. That's what Christ attacks in Matthew 5:43-44.

In the Sermon on the Mount, Jesus is saying this to the scribes and Pharisees: "No matter how intellectually convinced you are, your system is inadequate to redeem anyone. You are not God's poeple, and you have not met the standard. You are sinners." He offered Himself as the Savior, knowing that no one would come to Him unless he realized he needed a Savior.

Christ's sermon is a message about sin. The Jewish religious leaders thought that because they didn't murder or commit adultery, they weren't sinners. They believed their divorces were acceptable as long as they did the right paperwork. They thought that because they kept their word when they swore by the name of God, they were all right. They believed it was ok to retaliate on an equal basis when harmed. But Jesus said, "You're wrong. If you hate someone, that's just like murder. If you look at someone lustfully, that's the same as adultery. If you divorce for nonbiblical reasons, that's evil. And if you don't keep your word even when you don't swear by God, you've sinned." Christ undermined the security of the religious leaders' system. In Matthew 5:43-48 He says, "You think you love as you should. But your love is restricted to those within your group who agree with you, and you think you have license to hate everyone else. You don't even love your neighbors as you should because of your self-indulgent pride."

II. THE TEACHING OF THE OLD TESTAMENT

What did the Old Testament teach about loving others? Did it say to hate your enemy? No, it said to love your neighbor.

A. The Perverted Perspective (see pp. 46-47)

B. The Proper Perspective

1. Concerning the Canaanites (see pp. 47-48)

2. Concerning the imprecatory psalms (see pp. 48-51)

a) Examining the psalmist's words (see pp. 48-50)

In Psalm 139 David says, "Do not I hate them, O Lord, that hate thee? . . . I hate them with perfect hatred" (vv. 21-22). That is the only justifiable hatred in the Bible. It's based on the same attitude presented in Psalm 69:9, where David says, "Zeal of thine house hath eaten me up; and the reproaches of those who reproached thee are fallen upon me."

The Bible teaches that it's wrong to be angry, but there is such a thing as righteous indignation. Jesus says we're not to be angry with one another in Matthew 5:21-24, yet He whipped moneychangers out of the Temple in John 2:13-17. What's the difference between anger and righteous indignation? Jesus never got angry with those who personally offended Him, but He did get angry with those who defiled the glory of God. We have the right to react in indignation when God is dishonored, but we shouldn't retaliate when we're personally offended. That applies to enemies: We should have perfect, or righteous, hatred for those who are the enemies of God.

b) Examining the psalmist's attitude (see pp. 50-51).

Immediately after David said to God, "I hate [Your enemies] with perfect hatred" (Ps. 139:22), he said, "Search me, O God, and know my heart; try me, and know my thoughts; and see if there be any wicked way in me" (vv. 23-24). He was saying, "God, I hate Your enemies with a perfect hatred. If You search my heart, You will know my motive is Your glory, not vengeance over personal matters. Zeal for the holiness of God and the sacredness of His truth is a good thing. The Old Testament tolerates that kind of anger, but it doesn't tolerate personal resentment or hostility toward someone. There is no place in the Christian's life for personal hatred out of pride or prejudice, no matter what has been done to him.

The Jewish religious leaders define the word *neighbor* in Leviticus 19:18 narrowly, but the Bible defines it broadly. The Jewish religious leaders taught that a neighbor was one who believed what you believed. In John 7:49 they curse those who don't know the law. They despised the

Galileans, whom they considered ignorant. They loved only those within their own group. But the Old Testament doesn't teach us to hate our enemy. The Jewish leaders added that to accommodate their pride and prejudice.

Lesson

3. Concerning a friend's possessions

Deuteronomy 22 contains God's perspective on loving your neighbor in a broad sense. There we find some of the Levitical laws, the codes for Israel's behavior. Verse 1 says, "Thou shalt not see thy brother's ox or his sheep go astray, and withhold thy help from them; thou shalt in any case bring them again unto thy brother." If your brother has an animal that gets loose and goes astray, you are to immediately help return it.

Verse 2 says, "And if thy brother be not near unto thee, or if thou know him not, then thou shalt bring it unto thine own house, and it shall be with thee until thy brother seek after it, and thou shalt restore it to him again." If you found a stray sheep or an ox, and you didn't know whom it belonged to, you were to take and feed it until the owner claimed it. Verse 3 continues, "In like manner shalt thou do with his ass; and so shalt thou do with his raiment [cloak]; and with every lost thing of thy brother's, which he hath lost and thou hast found." You don't own something that someone loses; you are to keep it until the owner comes to claim it. That helps meet the owner's need.

Verse 4 states, "Thou shalt not see thy brother's ass or his ox fall down by the way, and withhold thy help from them; thou shalt surely help him to lift them up again." Sometimes when an animal became tired from carrying a heavy burden, it would fall down. It's difficult for someone to raise a large animal himself, so you were to assist someone in that situation. Although Deuteronomy 22:1-4 doesn't talk about loving your enemy, the principles can apply to that, as we will see in the next passage we look at.

4. Concerning an enemy's possessions

Exodus 23:4 says, "If thou meet thine enemy's ox or his ass going astray, thou shalt surely bring it back to him again." That's the same principle as the one in Deuteronomy 22, except in the latter, the term *brother* is used. Therefore the word *brother* has to encompass enemies. Exodus 23:5 says, "If thou see the ass of him that hateth thee lying under its burden, and wouldest forbear to help him, thou shalt surely help with him." If we saw our enemy's pack animal fall down, our normal reaction would be, "Serves you right, buddy! I hope your animal dies!" But the Old Testament says we are to help others, even our enemies.

God's standard doesn't change depending on who's involved; the terms *brother* and *neighbor* are broad enough to include whoever happens to have a need (Luke 10:25-37). The command to love your neighbor encompasses everyone; Psalm 119:96 says that the commandment of God "is exceedingly broad." We should love anyone who has a need, no matter how he feels about us. We're not talking about two nations at war, or a criminal who deserves punishment, but about our day-to-day human relationships.

5. Concerning an enemy's problems

When Job became afflicted with diseases and problems, his friends told him it was because he was a sinner. But God was using Job for a purpose; Job hadn't done anything wrong to bring about his bad circumstances. Yet his counselors thought he had and kept telling him so. One statement Job made to them that I'd like to look at appears in Job 31:29: "If I rejoiced at the destruction of him that hated me, or lifted up myself when evil found him." He was saying, "If I had rejoiced when an enemy of mine had fallen into evil, I would have sinned. You would have a right to accuse me if I had ever done that." Usually when an enemy has problems, our first reaction is to be happy. The worse the problem, the better we like it. That's human nature. But Job said, "Had I done that, I would have sinned."

In verse 30 Job says, "Neither have I suffered my mouth to sin by wishing a curse to his [my enemy's] soul." He never said an evil word to anyone. Many of us want to slander, curse, and condemn our enemies. Job never rejoiced when an enemy fell into calamity, nor did he wish evil on anyone. Verse 31 continues, "If the men of my tent said not, Oh, that we had of his flesh! We cannot be satisfied." In other words, "We've never longed for the flesh of an enemy. We've never been dissatisfied enough to want more harm to come to someone." Job had the right attitude toward his enemies. He lived in the patriarchal period, which goes back to the earliest years of God's dealing with man. From the very beginning, God's standard was one of love and forgiveness toward an enemy, not wishing evil upon him.

6. Concerning retaliation

a) Psalm 7:3-5

David prayed, "O Lord my God, if I have done this, if there be iniquity in my hands, if I have rewarded evil unto him who was at peace with me (yea, I have delivered him who without cause is mine enemy)" (vv. 3-4). David was talking about two things: It's wrong to be evil to those who are good to you and also to those who are evil to you. David said if he ever did that, "Let the enemy persecute my soul, and take it; yea, let him tread down my life upon the earth, and lay mine honor in the dust" (v. 5). David was right before God; he was saying, "I've looked at my heart, and have never given back evil for good or evil for evil." The Old Testament never justifies hating an enemy. That is a sin.

b) Psalm 35:12-16

In Psalm 35:12-13 David says of his enemies, "They rewarded me evil for good to the spoiling of my soul. But as for me, when they were sick, my clothing was sackcloth." When someone wore sackcloth, it meant he was full of remorse and sorrow. So David was saying, "When I was good to my enemies, they were cruel to me, but when evil fell upon them, I mourned over them. My heart was broken." That's the spirit Christ had when He hung on the cross, looked at those who spit on Him, and said, "Father, forgive them; for they know not what they do" (Luke 23:34). That's the attitude Stephen had when he was being stoned by his enemies, for he said, "Lord, lay not this sin to their charge" (Acts 7:60).

David expressed magnanimous, unbelievable forgiveness when his enemies repaid good with evil, and wore sackcloth when they suffered. He said, "I humbled my soul with fasting, and my prayer returned into mine own bosom. I behaved myself as though he [my enemy] had been my friend or brother" (Psalm 35:13-14). He says at the end of verse 14, "I bowed down heavily, as one who mourneth for his mother." He showed a dimension of love beyond the human level. Verses 15-16 continue, "In mine adversity they [my enemies] rejoiced, and gathered themselves together; yea . . . they did tear at me, and ceased not. With hypocritical mockers in feasts, they gnashed upon me with their teeth." But that wasn't the way David was toward his enemies.

c) Proverbs 17:5

Here we read, "Whoso mocketh the poor reproacheth his Maker; and he that is glad at calamities shall not be unpunished." If you rejoice when evil falls on someone, you won't go unpunished. That is a sin, even when the person in mind is an enemy.

d) Proverbs 24:29

The following is a command: "Say not, I will do so to him as he hath done to me." Don't retaliate; don't strike back at your enemy. That's the opposite of the golden rule.

Proverbs 25:21 sums up the Bible's teaching about the attitude we should have toward our enemies: "If thine enemy be hungry, give him bread to eat; and if he be thirsty, give him water to drink." Your enemy is your neighbor; that's what the Old Testament teaches. In a human sense, your enemy is your brother, although he isn't in a spiritual sense.

7. Concerning peaceful relations with enemies

a) Abram and Lot

(1) The situation

In Genesis 13, Abram and Lot have a dispute. Verses 5-7 say they had "flocks, and herds, and tents. And the land was not able to bear them, that they might dwell together; for their substance was great, so that they could not dwell together. And there was a strife between the herdsmen of Abram's cattle and the herdsmen of Lot's cattle."

(2) The response

How was the situation handled? Verses 8-9 tell us what Abram did: "Abram said unto Lot, Let there be no strife, I pray thee, between me and thee, and between my herdsmen and thy herdsmen; for we are brethren. Is not the whole land before thee? Separate thyself, I pray thee, from me: if thou wilt take the left hand, then I will go to the right; or if thou depart to the right hand, then I will go to the left." Now that is an amazing reaction. Abram ended the fight between him and Lot when he said, "Lot, you take whatever you want, and I'll just take what's left. You pick out the best and take it." That's how to treat an enemy; give him the best there is.

Verses 10-13 say, "Lot lifted up his eyes, and beheld all the plain of Jordan, that it was well watered everywhere, before the Lord destroyed Sodom and Gomorrah, even as the garden of the Lord, like the land of Egypt, as thou comest unto Zoar. Then Lot chose him all the plain of Jordan; and Lot journeyed east: and they separated themselves the one from the other. Abram dwelt in the land of Canaan, and Lot dwelt in the cities of the plain, and pitched his tent toward Sodom. But the men of Sodom were wicked and sinners before the Lord exceedingly." We could go on to talk about Lot's stupidity in pitching his tent toward Sodom, but the point we are to see here is that Abram treated Lot the way the Bible says we are to treat an enemy. He loved Lot as he loved himself. Instead of seeking the best land for himself, he sought the best for his enemy. The Bible honors that kind of virtue.

b) David and Saul

(1) The situation

First Samuel 24 begins, "And it came to pass, when Saul was returned from following the Philistines, that it was told him, saying, Behold, David is in the wilderness of Engedi" (v. 1). Up to this time, Saul had been chasing David because he was a threat to his throne. He was doing everything he could to murder David. When Saul was told that David was hiding in the wilderness of Engedi, he "took three thousand chosen men out of all Israel, and went to seek David and his men upon the rocks of the wild goats. And he came to the sheepcotes by the way [sheepcotes were little piles of rocks that were put in front of a cave to keep sheep inside], where was a cave, and Saul went in to cover his feet" (vv. 2-3).

The phrase "cover his feet "is a Hebrew expression for what we would call a visit to the men's room. In those days people wore long robes, and when they needed to perform the function of nature, they would get down on their haunches, and put their robe around them covering their feet. When Saul went into the cave to do that, he didn't know that David and his men were also in the same cave. Verse 3 says they were on the sides of the cave, and apparently Saul was in the middle.

When David's men saw Saul, they said to David, "Behold, the day of which the Lord said unto thee, Behold, I will deliver thine enemy into thine hand, that thou mayest do to him as it shall seem good unto thee" (v. 4). They said, "The Lord's prophecy has come true! Here's Saul, of all places, in the wilderness of Engedi, before us like a sitting duck. This is your chance to get him!" The rest of verse 4 says, "Then David arose, and cut off the skirt of Saul's robe stealthily." He cut off a piece of Saul's robe, although his men wanted him to kill Saul.

(2) The response

In verses 5-6 we read, "And it came to pass afterward, that David's heart smote him, because he had cut off Saul's skirt. And he said unto his men, The Lord forbid that I should do this thing unto my master, the Lord's anointed, to stretch forth mine hand against him, seeing he is the anointed of the Lord." We will feel convicted when we do evil to an enemy, for even our enemies are created and loved by God. Verses 7-8 continue, "So David restrained his servants with these words, and permitted them not to rise against Saul. But Saul rose up out of the cave, and went on his way. David also arose afterward, and went out of the cave, and cried after Saul, saying, My lord, the king. And when Saul looked behind him, David stooped with his face to the earth, and bowed himself." David paid homage to his enemy. He was a godly man, as was Abram. The virtuous man behaves toward an enemy as he would behave toward a friend, because an enemy is a neighbor.

c) David and Shimei

(1) The situation

David was not a very good father. He was too lenient with his son Absalom. Absalom later rebelled and wanted to usurp David's throne. The situation broke David's heart, and when Absalom was finally killed in battle, he wept and said, "Oh my son Absalom, my son, my son Absalom!" (2 Sam. 18:33).

Something interesting happened when David was fleeing from Absalom. Second Samuel 16:5-8 tells us, "When King David came to Bahurim, behold, there came out a man of the family of the house of Saul, whose name was Shimei, the son of Gera; he came forth, and cursed continually as he came. And he cast stones at David, and at all the servants of King David; and all the people and all the mighty men were on his right hand and on his left. And thus said Shimei when he cursed, Come out, come out, thou bloody man, and thou worthless fellow [apparently David was hidden among the people with him]; the Lord hath returned upon thee all the blood of the house of Saul, in whose stead thou hast reigned." Shimei was saying, "Do you know why your son Absalom has turned against you? Because you dethroned Saul. Now you're going to pay for what you did, you bloody man!" Shimei may have behaved the way he did because he was from Saul's family.

In verse 8 Shimei continues, "The Lord hath delivered the kingdom into the hand of Absalom, thy son; and, behold, thou art taken in thy mischief, because thou art a bloody man." Then in verse 9 one of David's men, Abishai, says to the king, "Why should this dead dog curse my lord, the king? Let me go over, I pray thee, and take off his head." To call someone a dead dog was very bad; that's probably the worst epithet Abishai could think of. Sometimes the Bible refers to pagans as dogs, and Peter referred to apostates as dogs who lick up their own vomit (2 Pet. 2:22). To call someone a dog was derogatory.

(2) The response

Abishai wanted to cut off Shimei's head, but the king said, "What have I to do with you, ye sons of Zeruiah [a reference to Abishai]? So let him curse, because the Lord hath said unto him, Curse David. Who shall then say, Why hast thou done so?" (v. 10). David thought perhaps the Lord had told Shimei to curse him. He was feeling the guilt of his failure with Absalom. Verses 11-14 say, "David said to Abishai, and to all his servants, Behold, my son, who came forth of my own body, seeketh my life: how much more, now, may this Benjamite do it? Let him alone, and let him curse; for the Lord hath bidden him. It may be that the Lord will look on mine affliction, and the Lord will requite me good for his cursing this day. And as David and his men went by the way, Shimei went along on the hillside opposite him, and cursed as he went, and threw stones at him, and cast dust. And the king, and all the people who were with him, became weary, and refreshed themselves there."

David's heart was right; he showed the kind of love the Old Testament teaches about. The Jews in Christ's day were wrong, for the Old Testament doesn't teach that we are to hate our enemies. They taught that to justify their evil prideful prejudices. The word *neighbor* in Leviticus 19:18 encompasses even enemies.

8. Concerning right responses toward persecution

In Matthew 5:10-12 Jesus says, "Blessed are they who are persecuted for righteousness sake; for theirs is the kingdom of heaven. Blessed are ye, when men shall revile you, and persecute you, and shall say all manner of evil against you falsely, for my sake. Rejoice, and be exceedingly glad." David is reacting with gladness to his persecution in 2 Samuel 16 when he says, in effect, "Perhaps the Lord will requite me someday for a right reaction to Shimei's cursing" (v. 12).

In every human relationship, God wants you to have the right reactions to whatever happens to you. Maybe you're experiencing conflict in your marriage, in your family, on the job, or perhaps some enemy is speaking against you. Those things will happen in this world. When an enemy speaks evil of us, our natural reaction will be one of hostility instead of love. Instead of seeing an enemy as our brother or neighbor, as the Old Testament does, we react bitterly toward him, and fall to the low level of pharisaic religion. That's not to be. The Old Testament tells us to love our enemies, and in Matthew 5:43-44, Jesus expresses absolute agreement with that principle.

III. THE TRUTH OF CHRIST

In Matthew 5:44 the Lord discusses the error of the Jewish religious system by giving five principles to correct the faulty love of the scribes and Pharisees. These principles are presented in an ascending manner: love your enemies, pray for your persecutors, manifest your sonship, exceed your fellow men, and imitate your God. The fifth principle in that list, more than any other, will help you to understand what Jesus meant when He said we're to love our enemies. It's the most powerful statement in the New Testament about the meaning of love.

A. Love Your Enemies

Matthew 5:44 says, "Love your enemies." Jesus spoke with authority when He said that; He is the Lord of the law and the Son of God.

An Emphatic Statement

In the Greek text of the New Testament, verbs change their form depending on what pronoun is used with them. You don't need pronouns like I, you, he, she, it, they, them, and your in Greek because the verb form indicates which pronoun is proper; it's at the end of the verb. When a pronoun is put in front of a verb, it intensifies the statement. It would have been sufficient for Christ to use the appropriate verb when He says, "I say unto you" in Matthew 5:44. But He used a pronoun before the verb, which put emphasis not on the saying but on Himself. By using the emphatic pronoun, He intensified the fact that He spoke authoritatively. He spoke as One who could speak over against the Jewish religious system regardless of what the renowned, astute teachers and rabbis in that system taught (Matt. 7:29). He is the Lord of the law.

1. The instruction

The Old Testament teaches that your enemy is your neighbor. Luke 10 illustrates that. There, a lawyer comes to Jesus and says, "Master, what shall I do to inherit eternal life? He [Christ] said unto him, What is written in the law? How readest thou? And he, answering, said, Thou shalt love the Lord thy God with all thy heart, and with all thy soul, and with all thy strength, and with all thy mind; and thy neighbor as thyself. And he [Christ] said unto him, Thou hast answered right; this do, and thou shalt live. But he, desiring to justify himself, said unto Jesus, and who is my neighbor?" (vv. 25-29). The lawyer was asking, "If you want me to love my neighbor, then who exactly is my neighbor?"

2. The illustration

Jesus answers the lawyer's question with a story beginning in verse 30: "A certain man went down from Jerusalem to Jericho, and fell among thieves, who stripped him of his raiment, and wounded him, and departed, leaving him half dead. And by chance there came down a certain priest that way; and when he saw him, he passed by on the other side" (vv. 30-31). A priest represented God to the people. Of all people in society, he should have behaved like God because he was His representative. But when the priest in Luke 10 sees the half-dead traveler, he doesn't want to touch him because he thinks the person might not be a neighbor—one of those in his own religious party. Then verse 32 says, "And likewise a Levite, when he was at the place, came and looked on him, and passed by on the other side." Both the Levite and the priest had nothing to do with the traveler.

In verse 33 Jesus continues, "But [then came] a certain Samaritan." The word *Samaritan* conjured all kinds of thoughts among the Jews of Christ's day, for they were a race that came from Jewish people who had intermarried with pagans from the Northern Kingdom in the Old Testament era. The Samaritans were half-breeds, and the most despicable thing to a Jew was for someone to defile himself by marrying a pagan. Jews refused to eat with Gentile utensils and didn't eat food cooked by a Gentile. They wouldn't go into Gentile houses because they believed the Gentiles aborted their babies in their homes, thus making them desecrated places. When they returned to Israel after traveling through Gentile countries, they would shake the dust off their garments because they didn't want to bring Gentile dust into their land. When they went from the south end of their land to the north, they crossed the Jordan River to the east, and then went north so they wouldn't have to pass through Samaria. They didn't want to defile themselves by passing through Samaria.

When the Samaritan comes across the half-dead traveler in Luke 10, his human response would have been, "My, look at the bleeding Jew. Good for him! It's about time one of them suffered, considering the way they've treated us!" But he didn't respond that way. The Jewish priest and Levite who had passed by the traveler earlier hadn't seen their own countryman as a neighbor, but the Samaritan did. Verses 34-35 say, "[The Samaritan] went to him, and bound up his wounds, pouring in oil and wine, and set him on his own beast, and brought him to an inn, and took care of him. And on the next day, when he departed, he took out two denarii, and gave them to the host, and said unto him, Take care of him; and whatever thou spendest more, when I come again, I will repay thee."

After Christ finished telling the story, He asked the lawyer, "Which, now, of these three, thinkest thou, was neighbor unto him that fell among the thieves? And he [the lawyer] said, he that showed mercy on him. Then said Jesus unto him, Go, and do thou likewise" (vv. 36-37).

Who is my neighbor? Anyone I meet who has a need is my neighbor, and not because he believes what I believe or because he's like me. God loved us and died for us when we were enemies (Rom. 5:10), and that's the kind of love we're to have for others.

Focusing on the Facts

1. Matthew presents Christ as what? How does he do that (see p. 55)?
2. What two problems are there with the Jewish rabbinical teaching, "Thou shalt love thy neighbor"? Explain (see pp. 56-57).
3. What is the difference between anger and righteous indignation (see p. 58)?
4. What biblical principle does Deuteronomy 22:1-4 teach (see p. 59)?
5. What is the difference between the content of Deuteronomy 22:1-4 and Exodus 23:4? What does that tell us (see pp. 59-60)?
6. Summarize what Job says in Job 31:29-31 (see pp. 60-61).
7. According to Psalm 35:12, how did David's enemies treat him? How did David treat his enemies (Ps. 35:13-14; see pp. 61-62)?
8. What does the book of Proverbs teach about how we should treat our enemies (see p. 62)?
9. What caused the strife between Abram and Lot? How did Abram handle that situation (see pp. 62-63)?
10. What commendable behavior did David show to his enemy Saul in 1 Samuel 24:7-8 (see pp. 63-65)?
11. Compare the responses of Abishai and David to Shimei's cursing in 2 Samuel 16 (see pp. 65-66).
12. How are we to respond to persecution (Matt. 5:12; see pp. 66-67)?
13. Christ uses a pronoun before the verb in Matthew 5:44 when He says, "I say unto you." What is He emphasizing (see pp. 67-68)?
14. What were the reactions of the priest and the Levite toward the half-dead traveler in the account of the good Samaritan (see p. 68)?
15. Explain the circumstances between the Jews and Samaritans in Christ's time. How did the Samaritan respond to the half-dead traveler in Luke 10:34-35 (see pp. 68-69)?
16. According to Luke 10:30-37, who is your neighbor (see p. 69)?

Pondering the Principles

1. Read 1 Peter 3:10-17. According to verse 10, what are we to refrain from? What does verse 11 say we are to seek? What is true about the righteous in verse 12? What attitude are we to have when we suffer for righteousness's sake (v. 14)? If we "sanctify the Lord God in [our] hearts, and are ready always to give an answer to every man that asketh [us] a reason of the hope that is in [us], with meekness and fear, having a good conscience" (vv. 15-16), what will be the result when our enemies slander us (v. 16)? What truth does Peter state in verse 17?

2. Reread the account of the good Samaritan in Luke 10:30-37. When Christ told the story, His listeners were probably surprised that the priest didn't stop to help the half-dead traveler. Christ was pointing out that although a person may profess to be religious, he is not a true child of God unless his actions confirm it. Read verses 34-35. On a scale of 1-10, how far out of his way did the Samaritan go to care for the Jewish traveler? On the same scale, how would you rate your love for your enemies? Think of how you have acted toward specific people. Spend some time in prayer right now, and ask Him to help you love your enemies.

5
Love Your Enemies— Part 3

Outline

Introduction
A. Discussing Godly Love
B. Demonstrating Godly Love
    1. Christ's example
    2. Stephen's example
    3. George Wishart's example

Review
  I. The Tradition of the Jewish Leaders
 II. The Teaching of the Old Testament
III. The Truth of Christ
    A. Love Your Enemies
       1. The instruction
       2. The illustration

Lesson
       3. The implementation
          a) Abandoning human love
          b) Applying biblical love
             (1) Demonstrating biblical love
             (2) Defining biblical love
    B. Pray for Your Persecutors
       1. The reason for persecution
       2. The response to our persecution
    C. Manifest Your Sonship
       1. Reflecting God's love
       2. Recognizing God's love
          a) His common love
          b) His covenantal love
    D. Exceed Your Fellow Man
       1. The inadequacy of conforming to man-made standards
       2. The importance of conforming to divine standards

E. Be Like God
   1. The inability of human effort
   2. The requirement for divine enablement

Introduction

We all have friends and enemies; we all know people who love to be with us and others who love to attack us. The test of our Christian character is not how we treat our friends, but how we treat our enemies. You can tell all there is to know about a man's true spirituality by what he does when people attack him. If he is a creature of love as a result of the indwelling presence of Jesus Christ, he will love his enemy as much as he loves his dearest friend. He will do that because it's his character to love, and his love will have little to do with the person involved.

A. Discussing Godly Love

   Jesus talks about loving our enemies in Matthew 5. In verse 43 He mentions that the Jewish religious leaders taught, "Thou shalt love thy neighbor, and hate thine enemy." They taught that to justify their hatred for their enemies. They said it was OK to be bitter and resentful toward someone, and that revenge was not wrong. The Jews were told by their teachers that prejudice was allowable and that there were some people you should hate. But Christ said, "I say unto you, Love your enemies" (v. 44). What people were doing and what God commanded were two different things. The people to whom Jesus spoke in the Sermon on the Mount thought they were good. But the Lord said, "You're not good at all! Your love is not adequate; it is very narrow. The love of those in My kingdom is indiscriminate. They love friends and enemies equally."

B. Demonstrating Godly Love

   1. Christ's example

      In Luke 23:34 we see a beautiful illustration of the love Christ was talking about. The Romans had done a foul deed: They had taken the Son of God, driven nails into His hands and feet, attached Him to a wooden cross, lifted the cross, and dropped it into its socket so that when it hit the bottom, the jolt would have torn His flesh. They spat upon Him and mocked Him. The Jewish leaders had also done a foul deed: They accused Christ of being a blasphemer, screamed for His blood, mocked

73

Him, and cast things in His face. When Christ hung on the cross, at His feet was a vicious, frenzied, hateful mob, thirsty for His blood. The crucifixion was the result of years of bitterness and hatred against One who was an agent of love.

Do you know how Christ reacted to His enemies? He said, "Father, forgive them; for they know not what they do" (Luke 23:34). Then the verse ends, "And they parted his raiment, and cast losts." In the midst of His magnanimous prayer of forgiveness, people were busy gambling for His cloak. Yet Jesus loved His enemies so much that He beseeched the Father for their forgiveness. His love was not human; mankind cannot produce such a love. You might say, "But Jesus was God. We can't love our enemies the way He did. That's beyond us." However, we can, as the next illustration shows us.

2. Stephen's example

Acts 6-7 tells of a man by the name of Stephen who was full of faith and of the Holy Spirit. He was among the first godly men chosen to oversee an important ministry in the church at Jerusalem. He knew God, the Old Testament, and the New Covenant under Christ. In Acts 7 he preaches a powerful, indicting sermon to a group of Jewish religious leaders, a message not unlike Peter's message on the day of Pentecost in Acts 2. He uncovered the sinfulness of Israel in his sermon, and by the time he was finished, his listeners were so frantic that they screamed and put their hands over their ears (v. 57). They picked him up, threw him over a precipice, and began to pummel his body with stones (v. 58). While he was being stoned, he pulled himself into a kneeling position to pray. What was his prayer? Simply this: "Lord, lay not this sin to their charge" (v. 60). He was saying, "Lord, be merciful. Don't make them pay for this; be gracious to them." That's what I call loving your enemies!

3. George Wishart's example

I have read the story of George Wishart, a sixteenth-century Scottish Reformer who was a martyr for his faith in Christ. He was to die because he loved Jesus and wouldn't deny Him. When he was taken to the place of execution, the executioner who was to take his life was burdened with guilt and was hesitant to put George to death because he knew his life and testimony. He asked

74

for Wishart's forgiveness. At that point Wishart asked the man to come forward, kissed him on the cheek, and said, "Here is a token that I forgive thee" (John Foxe, *Foxe's Book of Martyrs*, ed. W. Grinton Berry [Grand Rapids: Baker, 1978], p. 252). It's that kind of love for your enemies Christ is talking about in Matthew 5:44.

Citizens of the kingdom don't hate; they don't even hate their enemies. Rather, they manifest godliness and the virtue of a transformed life. The Jewish leaders thought they were all right, but the Lord showed them they weren't because of their inadequate, narrow love. So in Matthew 5:44-48, Jesus teaches the truth about love.

Review

I. THE TRADITION OF THE JEWISH LEADERS (see pp. 41-46, 56-57)

II. THE TEACHING OF THE OLD TESTAMENT (see pp. 57-67)

III. THE TRUTH OF CHRIST

In Matthew 5:44-48, there are five sequential truths that lead to a marvelous conclusion. Before we examine them, it's important to keep in mind Christ's audience.

Does the Sermon on the Mount Apply to Everyone?

Christ speaks with a twofold purpose in His Sermon on the Mount:

1. The application to unbelievers

   Suppose an unbeliever was listening to Christ's words. What would his reaction be? Christ wanted unbelievers to realize they fell short of God's standard because of the way they loved others. He wanted them to recognize that they were sinful. Upon seeing that, they would then realize their need for a Savior. Christ's message to the massive crowd of Jews before Him was this: "God's standard should prove to you that you aren't righteous and that you need a Savior."

2. The application to believers

   The disciples were the other group that was on the hillside when Jesus preached. They had already committed their lives to Him. But sometimes those who have been forgiven for their lack of love and given the power to love still don't love others as they should. To the disciples and other believers, then, the Lord's sermon becomes an exhortation to live up to what is now a potential reality.

So Christ was saying two things in His message; To one group of people He said, "If you don't love others the way you should, you're a sinner and you must be forgiven." To the other group He said, "If you have been forgiven and you've been given the capacity to love as you should, you must obey the command to love everyone." The Lord's message was for both believers and unbelievers. To believers it's an exhortation to a greater love, and for unbelievers it's an indictment of their sinfulness and need for a Savior.

A. Love Your Enemies (see pp. 67-69)

1. The instruction (see p. 68)

In Matthew 5:44 Jesus says, "I say unto you, Love your enemies." That was a devastating statement for the Lord to make to that society because there was so much hate there. Commentator William Hendricksen wrote, "All around [Jesus] were those walls and fences. He came for the very purpose of bursting those barriers, so that love— pure, warm, divine, infinite—would be able to flow straight down from the heart of God, hence from his own marvelous heart, into the hearts of men. His love over-leaped all the boundaries of race, nationality, party, age, sex, etc. When he said, 'I tell you, love your enemies,' he must have startled his audience, for he was saying something that probably never before had been said so succinctly, positively, and forcefully." (*The Gospel of Matthew* [Grand Rapids: Baker, 1973], p. 313).

Christ talked about something the people of His time didn't do. The Jewish religious leaders were proud and had many prejudices. They were judgmental, hateful men masquerading as religious people. Jesus devastated them when He said, "love your enemies," for that contradicted their life-style. The Jewish religious leaders hated the common people, the tax collectors who had sold out to Rome, and especially the Gentiles. Jesus' simple command laid bare their hate.

2. The illustration (see pp. 68-69)

Whom did Christ have in mind when He said, "Love your enemies"? Everyone. We saw in the previous lesson that the word *neighbor* encompassed enemies. From Luke 10 we learn that a neighbor is anyone in need. There, a Samaritan helps a half-dead Jewish traveler. That was surprising since the Samaritans and Jews hated each other. The Samaritan bound up the man's wounds, cared for him, put him on his own animal, and paid for his stay at an inn. That was a sacrifice of time, energy, money, and prejudice. He put aside the hatred his race had toward the Jews to help a man in need. Your neighbor is anyone in your path who has a need.

Prior to the telling of the story about the good Samaritan in Luke 10, a lawyer had asked Jesus, "Who is my neighbor?" (Luke 10:29). It was as if he was saying, "I want to pick out my neighbors and then I'll love them as I should." But when Christ finished with the story about the good Samaritan, He said, "Which, now, of these three, thinkest thou, was neighbor unto him that fell among the thieves?" (v. 36). First a priest had gone by the traveler, but he ignored him. Then a Levite, a priest's helper, passed by. Neither of the religious men helped the traveler. But then the Samaritan came along and helped the traveler. When Christ asked the lawyer which person proved to be a neighbor to the traveler, He was saying, "Instead of going through life picking out your neighbors, you are to be a neighbor to everyone you meet."

Lesson

3. The implementation

   a) Abandoning human love

   In our society, people are object-oriented in their love. They love others on the basis of whether someone attracts them or not. Men, when looking for a woman to marry, will look for certain characteristics. They will bypass many of the women they meet, but when they come across the right woman, they'll zero in on her. We generally base our love for someone on our feelings for that person. Thus, our love is object-oriented. When we look at pictures, houses, or cars, some will attract us and some won't. Some personalities attract our love and others don't. That's the way human affection is. The lawyer in Luke 10 is the same way; he was wondering whom he should attach himself to as a neighbor. But Jesus said that's not the issue. You should be a neighbor to everyone. Any person in your path should receive your love. Don't try to figure out who your neighbor is; be a neighbor to everyone, then you won't have a problem. Christ called for us to love our enemies. That means we are to love everyone equally, whether he is a friend or not.

b) Applying biblical love

When Christ was talking about loving your enemies, He wasn't talking about affection. He doesn't expect you to love them with the love of friendship (Gk., *philia*) or with familial love (Gk., *storgē*). He doesn't expect you to love your enemies with an affectionate love (Gk., *erōs*); rather, He wants you to show them *agapē* love, a love that seeks the good of others and meets their needs.

(1) Demonstrating biblical love

In John 13:34, after Jesus washes the disciples' feet, He tells them to love one another as He has loved them. However, He didn't say that because the disciples were so wonderful and irresistible. In fact, they were cantankerous; they had been arguing over who would be the greatest in the kingdom of heaven (Luke 22:24). They had been acting sinfully and were self-centered. They weren't even considerate enough to comfort Christ prior to His death on the cross. Yet even though they had been acting that way, He said, "love each other as I have loved you." How did He show His love to them? He washed their dirty feet. Love is an act of service to one in need, not necessarily an emotion.

After the Lord says, "Love your enemies" in Matthew 5:44, He adds, "Bless them that curse you, do good to them that hate you, and pray for them who despitefully use you, and persecute you." (That doesn't appear in the better Greek manuscripts; Christ does say that in Luke 6:27-28 and probably it was been brought over to Matthew 5 by a scribe.) What Jesus was saying is true. If you love your enemy, you'll bless him when he curses you, and you'll do good to him

78

when he does evil to you. That's the outworking of your love for your enemy. It's not so much your feelings that God is concerned about, but what you say and do. You might not have any affection for an enemy. You know there will never be a true friendship between you and him. But you are to bless him in what you say and do. The love Christ is talking about in Matthew 5:44 is one of action, not of emotion.

(2) Defining biblical love

First Corinthians 13 has perhaps the greatest definition of love ever given. In verses 4-7 are fifteen characteristics of love, and all appear as verbs. That's because love is an action. It can't be defined statistically or as a plateau. It's always active. Someone once said 1 Corinthians 13:4-7 is a lyrical interpretation of the Sermon on the Mount because of the parallel between the two sections of Scripture. When Paul described love, he used verbs because love is described only in terms of what it does. You may have had trouble believing certain people who say they love you because their actions don't support their words. You have every right to question that kind of love because love does things.

Verse 4 says, "Love is patient" (NASB*), which means "long-tempered." The word *long-tempered* is used to speak of patience with people. Next, love "is kind." In the Greek text, the word translated *kind* means "useful." Love does deeds of kindness that help people in times of need. Love also "envieth not." It doesn't have a competitive spirit, nor is it jealous. It joys in another's success. Love "vaunteth not itself." The Greek term refers to outward bragging or showing off. We also read that love "is not puffed up." That refers to being self-centered.

In verse 5 Paul says love "doth not behave itself unseemly." Love is not rude. It's always concerned about people and dealing with them tenderly. It never insists on its rights. Today you can take week-long seminars on how to assert your

New American Standard Bible.

rights. But that's not the way love acts. Next, love "seeketh not its own." A loving person will be unselfish and seek the good of others. Love also is "not easily provoked." A person who is loving doesn't go into sudden outbursts of anger or rage. He won't react to injury or lose his temper. Verse 5 ends by saying that love "thinketh no evil." Love always thinks the best of others. It forgives and forgets, and doesn't carry grudges. It's never defensive or eager to blame someone else.

Verse 6 tells us that love "rejoiceth not in iniquity." It never takes pleasure when someone else sins or is chastised. Rather, it "rejoiceth in the truth." Love is positive and encouraging. Then verse 7 adds that love "beareth all things, believeth all things, hopeth all things, [and] endureth all things." In the Greek text, bearing all things means throwing a blanket on another person's faults and covering them. Love is never suspicious; it always believes the best. Love hopes; even when it knows the prospect of failure, it is still optimistic. It doesn't accept failure as final. And last, love endures all things, no matter what happens. In verse 8 Paul says, "Love never faileth."

Paul's description of love is like a prism that displays all the colors of love. The love he talked about is the kind of love that characterizes our Lord Jesus Christ. Do you love like that? If you don't, you need a Savior. If you've already received His forgiveness for your lack of love, Christ lives in your heart and "the love of God is shed abroad" in you (Rom. 5:5). If you aren't letting that love out, then you need to make a new commitment to love others the way God wants you to.

Bible commentator R. C. H. Lenski said, "[Love] indeed, sees all the hatefulness and the wickedness of the enemy, feels his stabs and his blows, may even have something to do toward warding them off; but all this fills the loving heart with the one desire and aim, to free its enemy from his hate, to rescue him from his sin, and thus to save his soul. Mere affection is often blind, but even then it thinks that it sees something attractive in the one toward whom it goes out; the higher love may see nothing attractive in the one so loved. . . its inner motive is simply to bestow true blessing on the one loved, to do him the highest good. . . . I cannot like a low, mean criminal who may have robbed me and threatened my life; I cannot like a false, lying, slanderous fellow who, perhaps, has vilified me again and again; but I can by the grace of Jesus Christ love them all, see what is wrong with them, desire and work to do them only good, most of all to free them from their vicious ways" *(The Interpretation of St. Matthew's Gospel* [Minneapolis: Augsburg, 1964], p. 247).*

We are to love our enemies not in terms of a feeling but in terms of service. In Romans 12:20 Paul says, "If thine enemy hunger, feed him; if he thirst, give him drink; for in so doing thou shalt heap coals of fire on his head." When you do good to your enemy, you convict him and make him feel bad about his hatred and sin. Verse 21 continues, "Be not overcome by evil, but overcome evil with good." When someone does evil to you, don't retaliate. Nothing your enemy does should make you fall into sin. Rather, your goodness should drown out his evil. Chrysostom, the fourth-century church Father, said that just as the sea extinguishes a spark, so does the love of a believer extinguish an injury. When people cast their sparks of hatred at us, they should be quenched by our love.

B. Pray for Your Persecutors

At the end of Matthew 5:44 Christ says, "Pray for them who despitefully use you, and persecute you." You are to beseech God on behalf of those who despitefully abuse and persecute you. When someone does evil to you or harms you, go before the Lord on his behalf and intercede for him. That's what Jesus did on the cross (Luke 23:34) and Stephen did when he was stoned (Acts 7:60). I've read many stories about Christians who, when they were put to death for the faith, would pray for those who were persecuting them. We can follow their example in small matters as well.

*Reprinted by permission from *The Interpretation of St. Matthew's Gospel,* by R. C. H. Lenski, copyright Augsburg Publishing House.

1. The reason for persecution

   There is no persecution or hatred as severe as that directed toward the people of God. That's because man lives with sin and guilt, which produces fear, and the ultimate fear man has is death. People ask themselves, "If there is a God and I have sinned, will I be punished?" Man lives with the imminence of punishment and thus lives in fear. Consequently, he constructs systems that help him deal with that fear. Some people convince themselves that if they keep enough rules, they will be OK and God will let them into heaven. Others say, "I am not guilty of anything. I will not fear the possibility of judgment. I can eliminate any such fear by saying there is no God."

   When you tell someone, "You're a sinner. You will die and go to hell apart from Christ. You need to be redeemed," you will strike him at the core of his deepest pain, because you are reminding him of all the guilt and fear over his sin that he has managed to sublimate under his philosophy or religion. Unmasking people at their most vulnerable point can result in the most severe persecution. Persecution also brings to focus the reality of the battle between Satan and God.

   When we truly stand up and live for Christ in our society, we will be persecuted. Yet in the midst of the worst kind of hatred and the worst persecution, we are to pray for those who seek to destroy us. What are we to pray for? I believe we are to beseech God for our persecutor's highest good. I don't think God wants us to pray for fire to come down from heaven and consume our enemies! We're to pray for our enemy's salvation.

2. The response to our persecution

   Nineteenth-century English preacher Charles Spurgeon said, "Prayer is the forerunner of mercy." When we pray, we release God's mercy in a very real way. That's what Jesus had in mind when He said, "Pray for your persecutors; pray for those who would take your life." It's easy for us to point to our enemies and say, "They are enemies of Christ, the cross, the Bible, and the church." We can easily think that because they represent what we hate, we have justification to hate them. But we are to love them; we are to hate the sin but love the sinner.

Wouldn't it be great if we prayed for the redemption of those who are set against us? Praying that way will fill your heart with love and wash your soul. When someone comes to me and says, "I have a problem with so-and-so, and I resent him," my response is always the same: Set aside a certain time every day to pray for that person." When you pray for God to be merciful to an enemy, you will wash your soul of bitterness. In fact, in one of his homilies on the gospel of Matthew, Chrysostom said that such a prayer is the highest summit of self-control. When you pray for your persecutors, you bring your life into conformity with God's standards.

Theologian Dietrich Bonhoeffer, who suffered much in Nazi Germany, said, "This is the supreme command. Through the medium of prayer we go to our enemy, stand by his side and plead to God for him" (*The Cost of Discipleship* [New York: Macmillan, 1960], p. 166). The cruel torture of crucifixion didn't silence Christ's prayer for His enemies, and the stones that crushed Stephen didn't silence his prayer. Has anything silenced your prayers for your enemies?

C. Manifest Your Sonship

Matthew 5:45 begins with the Greek word *hopōs*, which indicates purpose. Why are we to love our enemies and pray for our persecutors? "That ye may be the sons of your Father" (v. 45). The aorist tense of the phrase translated "may be" renders the statement, "So that it may become once and for all an established fact that you are a son of God."

1. Reflecting God's love

The Bible says, "God is love" (1 John 4:16). If God is love, and I'm His child, I should be characterized by love. First John 4:20 says, "If a man says, I love God, and hateth his brother, he is a liar." Don't claim you belong to God if you don't manifest love. Now Christ wasn't saying in Matthew 5:44-45 that you can become a son of God by loving your enemies. He was saying, "You will prove the validity of your claim to be a son of God when love is manifest in your life." As Peter says in his second epistle, we are "partakers of the divine nature" (1:4), but to make our calling and election sure we have to add virtue and other things to what we've already received (1:5-10). We will never convince anyone we belong to God unless we're like Him. Manifest your sonship.

Tarnishing the Image

When I was a little boy, a friend and I once got into trouble when we were caught stealing some things from a Sears store. We were taken to the city jail in Glendale. At the time, my father was out playing golf with some deacons from our church. He was notified about what had happened and came to the jail thinking a mistake had been made. Then he had to explain to the deacons what his son was doing in jail. When I got home, my mother was crying because she thought I would never do such a thing. One person said, "Johnny MacArthur, have you forgotten who your father is?" I never forgot that statement. I owed something to my father. He had given me my very life, and I was happy I was his son.

One of my sons once asked me, "Dad, are you ever going to retire?" I said no. He said, "Good, because I'm glad you're a preacher." I asked him, "Are you glad to be my son?" He said yes. I'm glad to be my Father's son too, but it's only right that I manifest something of my Father's character.

The scribes and Pharisees in Christ's time claimed to be the sons of God, but they didn't manifest the character of God. Do you know the biggest excuse some people have for rejecting the truth of the gospel? The people who claim to live it but don't. There are many hypocrites in the church. The biggest detriment to Christianity is Christians who don't live up to the standard they ascribe to. We are to manifest our sonship.

There are people around us who are Christians but who never show it because they don't love others as they should. But when the world sees someone whose life is full of love for everyone whether he is a friend or not, it will have a difficult time assuming that love comes from a human source. People don't normally love like that. When Jesus said we are to be the sons of our Father in heaven, He was saying that our life-style shouldn't reflect a worldly source but a heavenly one. Our Father is a heavenly father, not an earthly one. We should be good in not just a philanthropic sense, but in a heavenly sense.

2. Recognizing God's love

   a) His common love

   Christ didn't just say we're to love as God loves; He gave us an illustration. Matthew 5:45 says, "He maketh His sun to rise on the evil and on the good, and sendeth rain on the just and on the unjust." First

Christ mentioned the evil before the good, then He mentioned the just before the unjust. He switched the order of those He was speaking about to show impartiality. God loves everyone. When the sun comes up in shining splendor and warmth, everyone benefits from it. When there is rain, it falls on everyone.

Some time ago I had the joy of being outside on a particularly beautiful afternoon and evening at a football game my son played in. There were three rainbows in the sky that day and big, puffy clouds everywhere. Then the moon came out, and later on a little rain trickled down. All the spectators who were at the football game enjoyed that evening too, even those who didn't know the Lord.

Every day, the sun gives the world light. It helps the grass in your yard to grow, and it nurtures the grass in the yards of those who don't acknowledge that God even exists. Why? Because God is good; He is indiscriminate in His benevolence. That's what the sixteenth-century French theologian John Calvin called common grace. Divine love and providence touches everyone. In Matthew 5:45 Christ is saying that we are to let our love be so indiscriminate that our sun shines on everyone and our rain falls on the just and unjust. When our love is like the Father's, it will be obvious that we belong to Him.

There's an old rabbinic tale that when the Egyptian army was drowned in the Red Sea, the angels began to praise God. But God lifted His hands mournfully, silenced the angels, and said, "The work of My hands are sunk in the sea, and you would sing before Me!" God loved Pharaoh and his soldiers, because He is love. Manifest your sonship by praying for your persecutors and loving your enemies. Psalm 145:15-16 says, "The eyes of all wait upon thee; and thou givest them their food in due season. Thou openest thine hand, and satisfieth the desire of every living thing." God is the source of the supplies for every living thing.

b) His covenantal love

All men receive common grace and providential love. But not everyone receives the special love God reserves for His covenant people. (In the Old Testament, the covenant people were the Israelites; under the New Covenant, they are those saved by the blood of Christ.) For example, Abraham had two sons, Ishmael and Isaac. Ishmael was an illegitimate son, not the covenant son God had planned for the messianic line. Yet in Genesis 17:20 God says, "As for Ishmael . . . I have blessed him, and will make him fruitful, and will multiply him exceedingly; twelve princes shall he beget, and I will make him a great nation." God was gracious even to Abraham's illegitimate son, an outcast. Verse 21 continues, "But my covenant will I establish with Isaac." God loved Ishmael, but He had a special love for Isaac. Likewise, He loves everyone in the world, but He has something special for His covenant people who come in faith to Christ. God's common grace and providential love are wonderful, but they won't save you. For salvation, you must come to Christ.

D. Exceed Your Fellow Man

1. The inadequacy of conforming to man-made standards

Christ says in Matthew 5:46, "If ye love them who love you, what reward have ye?" If you just go around loving those who belong to your circle of friends, are you to be commended? Are you to receive some kind of reward? Our Lord said, "Do not even the tax collectors the same?" It would be difficult for us to imagine the emotional feelings that the scribes and Pharisees had when Christ said that. If there was any group they hated, it was the tax collectors in their society. They were renegade Jews who had committed treason against Israel by extorting taxes for themselves and the Roman government. In the Roman Empire, a Roman citizen could buy rights to tax the people who lived in a certain territory. In Israel, money-minded Jews were often hired by such citizens to collect the taxes. The tax collector only had to collect a certain amount, and with anything else he got, he padded his own pockets. Thus tax collectors were despised; that is made evident in Matthew, Mark, and Luke.

Jesus told the Jewish religious leaders, "If you love just the people who share your prejudices and think the same way you do, you're no better than traitors, renegades, and publicans because they love those who are in their groups too. Your kind of love doesn't prove you belong in My kingdom." The Pharisees had said, "We show love to those within our group," and Jesus replied, "The worst people in the human race do the same thing." Murderers, thieves, adulterers, and extortioners love those who have something in common with themselves. I once read that some people who are released from prison can't wait to get back because that's where their friends are. Some people commit crimes repeatedly because they are more at home in jail than they are outside of it. You're no better than anyone else if all you can do is love the people in your own group.

If what Jesus said in Matthew 5:46 was a blow, what He said in verse 47 infuriated the Jewish religious leaders even more: "If ye greet your brethren only, what do ye more than others? Do not even the heathen [Gentiles] so?" The word "greet" in that verse has to do with a warm embrace and a kiss, a custom which is still practiced in the Middle East. Christ was saying, "If you give a warm and affectionate embrace for your brothers only, you're no better than a Gentile. Now a Gentile was considered even worse than a tax collector. When Jesus said the Jewish religious leaders were no better than tax collectors and Gentiles, He must have upset them. He told them that those who lived under their form of religion were no better than anyone else.

2. The importance of conforming to divine standards

The key statement in Matthew 5:47 is, "What do ye more than others?" Our Lord was saying, "If you don't exceed the human standard, you're no different than anyone else. Why should you be rewarded for being like everyone else? Why should God reserve His crowns for you and pour out His blessings on you?" It was devastating for Christ to say that the religious people were no better than the heathen, and that the people who worked in the Temple were no better than those who extorted money. He said, "You're all sinners. You only differ in the way you sin. You religious leaders are no better than anyone else!" We have to ask ourselves the same question Jesus posed to them: What makes us different from those who are in the world? Are we different because of our ethics, conversation, attitudes, and love? Are we different only in the kinds of homes and communities we live in? If we're not different, others will not believe what we say about Christianity because our actions won't back us up.

Author J. Oswald Sanders said that the Master expects from His disciples such conduct as can be explained only in terms of the supernatural. If your conduct can be explained only in those terms, then society will take note of what you say. But if you're like everyone else, people will say, "What do you have to offer that I don't have?" The only way we will be able to call the godless people of this age to Christ is if our lives are unique and there is no explanation for them except that God is in us.

E. Be Like God

1. The inability of human effort

The culmination of Christ's teaching in Matthew 5 is: "Be ye, therefore, perfect" (Matt. 5:48). Some people think He was only saying we are to become mature; we are to be growing. But He said, "Be ye, therefore, *perfect*, even as your Father, who is in heaven, is *perfect*" (Matt. 5:48; emphasis added). The point is that you are to be like God. You say, "The standard is too high!" That's right, and that's exactly what Jesus wanted the Pharisees to realize. You can't get into the kingdom on your own. He wanted them to admit they couldn't be perfect.

2. The requirement for divine enablement

If you fall short of perfection, you need a Savior. When you receive Jesus into your life, you become a partaker of the divine nature (2 Pet. 1:4). In the miracle of salvation, God does for you what you could never do yourself: He helps you to be like Him. If you have already come to Christ, you have received eternal life and righteousness in a positional sense. Now you have to make sure your behavior is in harmony with your position. A Christian is not someone who keeps the Sermon on the Mount; he is someone who knows he can't do that. He comes to Christ asking for forgiveness because he falls short of God's standard. Christ then forgives him and gives him the power to begin to live out the Sermon on the Mount. And even when you fail, you're forgiven, because Christ has already paid the price for your sins.

What is Christ saying in Matthew 5 about loving our enemies? If you don't love the way you should, that's a sin. And since you're a sinner, you need a Savior. Jesus is willing to come into your life and forgive your sin of lovelessness. He will cleanse your life, plant His love in your heart, and teach you how to love the way He wants you to love. For some of you, Christ's message is a call to salvation; to others, it's an exhortation to let the love within you flow outward to others. Jesus calls us to love with a love that shows no discrimination. Such love will show that we're like God, and will reveal Him to others. That is how to become effective evangelists. May God help us to love the others so that we manifest His nature.

Focusing on the Facts

1. Why will a person who is indwelt by Christ love an enemy as much as he loves a friend (see p. 73)?
2. What did the Romans and the Jewish religious leaders do to Christ when He was crucified (see pp. 73-74)? What was Christ's response (see pp. 73-74)?
3. Explain what kind of response Christ wanted from the unbelievers who heard the Sermon on the Mount. What was Christ's message to the believers who heard Him speak (see p. 76)?
4. What did the Samaritan in Luke 10 sacrifice when he helped the half-dead Jewish traveler (see p. 77)?
5. On what basis do people in our society love others? Explain (see p. 77).
6. What kind of love should you have for your enemies (see p. 78)?
7. Describe what ought to be the outworking of your love for your enemy (Matt. 5:44; see pp. 78-79).
8. Describe the definition of love as it is given in 1 Corinthians 13:4-7 (see p. 79).
9. What did Bible commentator R. C. H. Lenski say about "mere affection" and "higher love" (see pp. 80-81)?
10. Why is the most intense persecution in the world directed toward God's people (see p. 80)?
11. Christ said to pray for those who persecute you. What are we to pray for specifically (see p. 82)?
12. What will praying for your enemies do to you (see p. 83)?
13. Why are we to love our enemies and pray for our persecutors (see p. 83)?
14. What is the biggest detriment to Christianity (see p. 84)?
15. What will happen when the world sees someone who loves both friends and enemies (see p. 84)?
16. Discuss what Christ was talking about when He said that God "maketh his sun to rise on the evil and on the good, and sendeth rain on the just and on the unjust" (Matt. 5:45; see pp. 84-85).

17. Explain the difference between God's common love and covenantal love (see pp. 85-86).
18. Why did Jesus say the Jewish religious leaders were no better than tax collectors and Gentiles (see pp. 86-87)?
19. What is the key statement in Matthew 5:47 (see p. 87)? What questions must we ask ourselves in relation to that, and why (see p. 87)?
20. What did Christ want people to recognize when He said, "Be ye, therefore, perfect" (Matt. 5:48; see p. 88)?
21. Discuss how divine enablement is required for living according to God's standard (see p. 88).

Pondering the Principles

1. Reread the section about the biblical definition of love from 1 Corinthians 13:4-7 on pages 78-79. With each characteristic of love mentioned, ask yourself the following questions: Am I currently putting this characteristic into practice in my life? Are there any opportunities for me to manifest this characteristic sometime in the next week or two? When you make a commitment to love others the way God wants you to, you will please God.

2. Read 1 John 4:7-21. What does verse 7 command us to do? What does verse 8 say about a person who doesn't love others? According to verses 9-10, how did God show His love to us? With that in mind, how much would you say God loves us? What parallel does John then make in verse 11? What truths do we learn from verse 16? What is the origin of the love we have for God (v. 19)? How does John conclude his discussion on love in verses 20-21?

6
Love Fulfills the Law—
Part 1

Outline

Introduction
A. The Call to Obey
B. The Capacity to Obey

Lesson
I. The Debt of Love (v. 8*a*)
   A. The Parallel: Owing Money
      1. Passages on loaning money
      2. Principles for loaning money
   B. The Principle: Owing Love
      1. The exhortation to love
      2. The elements of love
         a) Love teaches others the truth of God
         b) Love ministers to the needs of others
         c) Love serves others and causes them to grow
         d) Love covers the sins of others
         e) Love forgives
         f) Love endures
         g) Love sacrifices for others
      3. The exercise of love
         a) Understand the resource
         b) Submit to the Holy Spirit
         c) Purify your heart
         d) Possess a sense of urgency
         e) Consciously choose to love others
         f) Interact with other believers
         g) Concentrate on others
         h) Consider the results

Introduction

Michael Griffiths, who has written some very insightful books on missions, once said that enthusiasm is easier than obedience. The apostle Paul would have probably said amen to that. In Romans 7 he says, "We know that the law is spiritual; but I am carnal, sold under sin. For that which I do I understand not; for what I would, that do I not; but what I hate, that do I. . . . For the good that I would, I do not; but the evil which I would not, that I do" (vv. 14-15, 19). Paul would have agreed that enthusiasm is easier than obedience. No matter how much we want to obey God, we sometimes find it difficult to do that. Even when we are eager to do God's will, we find ourselves bound by our humanness and unable to do all the good that we desire to do.

A. The Call to Obey

Even though it's difficult to always be obedient, it's an essential element of Christianity. If I were to define the Christian life with one word, I would choose the word *obedience*. We are to follow the truth and the Spirit of God, obeying His Word. Obedience, power, blessing, and joy are four legs to the same chair; they are essential elements of the Christian life. Without obedience to God, there will be no power, blessing, or joy in our lives. There are some people who say we must let go of everything and let God take care of it all. It's true we have to allow the Spirit and power of God to work through us, but we must expend effort on our part to be obedient.

One key distinction between a true Christian and someone who merely professes to be a Christian is a heartfelt desire to obey God. That is the truest indicator we find of the authenticity of Paul's conversion in Romans 7. For a Christian, *obedience* is a sweet, hopeful, and encouraging word. It is a welcome expression of the deepest desire in the heart of a believer. Obedience marks the attitude of a true child of God. He has a heart that is willing to obey, and his desire to do so comes out of love, not fear.

Some people say, "Since we are saved by grace (Rom. 5), and are no longer under the law (Rom. 6), then aren't we no longer bound to the law?" Yes in one sense, but no in another. We are not bound to the penalty of the law. Since we came to Christ, the law no longer has power to condemn or execute us. However, we are bound to its precepts, for God has not changed His morality. He hasn't abandoned His standard of truth. Romans 8:1-3 says, "There is, therefore, now no condemnation to them who are in Christ Jesus. . . . For the law of the Spirit of life in Christ Jesus hath made [us] free from the law of sin and death. For what the law could not do, in that it was weak through the flesh, God sending his own Son, in the likeness of sinful flesh and for sin, condemned sin in the flesh."

B. The Capacity to Obey

The sacrifice of Christ freed us from the penalty of the law. He died in our place. Verse 4 tells us the purpose of redemption: "That the righteousness of the law might be fulfilled in us, who walk not after the flesh, but after the Spirit." Because a Christian walks in the Spirit, he has the capacity to fulfill the law. So we are free from the law only in the sense that it can't condemn us, yet we are still commanded to obey its precepts.

With that in mind, the question comes up: How can we keep the law? If we are called to obedience and our new nature longs to obey, what are we to do when we find ourselves tempted to disobey? It's true we have the power of the Spirit in us (Rom. 8:2), which enables us to do the will of God. But Romans 7 tells us that we will still battle with the flesh. Verse 23 says we have "another law in [our] members, warring against the law of [our] mind." The sin principle in our humanness wars against our desire to obey. Every Christian fights that battle. Your humanness wars against the new creation that delights in the law of God. What gives us hope is that the longer we fight the battle, the more victorious we will be. We will learn to gain victory even before the Lord comes to deliver us from the constraints of our humanness.

If you are a true Christian, you will desire to obey God. You will long to do right, as Paul did in Romans 7, yet you will sometimes be restrained by your flesh. How can you overcome that? What is the key to obedience? Let's see if we can answer that question in our study of Romans 13.

Lesson

Beginning in Romans 12, Paul talks about the practical ramifications of being justified. The results of our salvation include a right relationship to God (v. 1), to the world (v. 2), and to the church (vv. 3-8). In Romans 13:1-7, Paul discusses a right relationship to the government, and here in verses 8-10, a right relationship to society. The way we relate to people is one of the many things that is affected by our salvation. Romans 12-13 basically deals with the outflowing of right relationships as a result of our redemption.

In Romans 13:8-10 Paul says the key to relationships within society is love. And love is the key to obedience. If you're a Christian, your heart's desire is to obey God, yet sometimes your flesh restrains you. How can you overcome that? Through love. Twice in Romans 13:8-10 Paul says that love fulfills the law. So he reduces obedience to one key concept: love. When I was young, I heard a man say, "The Christian life can be lived like this: Love everyone perfectly and do whatever you want." At first that didn't make much sense to me, even though it sounded good. But now I understand what he meant, and I think you will too as we look at Romans 13:8-10 a little more closely.

Love is the key in the relationships discussed in Romans 12-13. In Romans 13:8-10 Paul says love is the key to everything in the Christian life. There are three basic things he covers: the debt of love, the discharge to love, and the design of love.

I. THE DEBT OF LOVE (v. 8a)

A. The Parallel: Owing Money

Romans 13:8 begins with these words: "Owe no man any thing, but to love one another." What did Paul mean by, "Owe no man any thing"? In verses 6-7 he had just talked about taxes, and the phrase at the beginning of the verse 8 is a bridge from the previous text. After talking about the importance of paying taxes, it's natural for him to say that we are to pay all our debts. He makes a transition from money owed to the government to debts owed to anyone in general. The imperative tense in the Greek text implies that the command applies to every relationship we have. No believer is to have unpaid debts. We are not to owe anyone anything.

Upon reading Romans 13:8, many people have asked, "Does that mean we should not borrow or take money on interest? Are we forbidden to borrow at any time for any reason?" Let's look at the Bible's answer to that.

1. Passages on loaning money

a) Exodus 22:25

In Exodus 22 God establishes some societal laws for his nation Israel. In verse 25 we read, "If thou lend money to any of my people who is poor among you, thou shalt not be to him as an usurer, neither shalt thou lay upon him usury." *Usury* is an old English

94

word that refers to exhorbitant interest. Today there are people who will consolidate all your debts for you, but then they charge an interest rate that will choke you. When you come across someone in need who has to borrow money from you, you're to lend it to them without charging exhorbitant interest. So based on that passage, it's all right to lend money, which means it's also all right to borrow it if you have needs you can't meet.

b) Deuteronomy 15:7-11

Verses 7-9 say, "If there be among you a poor man of one of thy brethren within any of thy gates in thy land which the Lord thy God giveth thee, thou shalt not harden thine heart, nor shut thine hand from thy poor brother; but thou shalt open thine hand wide unto him, and shalt surely lend him sufficient for his need, in that which he lacketh. Beware that there be not a thought in thy wicked heart, saying, The seventh year, the year of release, is at hand; and thine eye be evil against thy poor brother."

Every seventh year in Israel, all debts were cancelled and land was not to be used for farming. When a poor person asked someone for money, sometimes the prospective lender would think, "I'd better not loan any money out now. Next year is the year of release, and I would have to cancel the debt. I'll never get paid back." But God said not to do that. If someone is in need of money, lend it to him. Verses 10-11 say, "Thou shalt surely give him, and thine heart shall not be grieved when thou givest unto him; because for this thing the Lord thy God shall bless thee in all thy works, and in all that thou puttest thine hand unto. For the poor shall never cease out of the land; therefore I command thee, saying, Thou shalt open thine hand wide unto thy brother, to thy poor, and to thy needs, in thy land."

Lending money was an important matter in the Old Testament era. If a farmer's crop didn't grow or someone lost his money through unwise investments or robbery, you were to loan them money. Lending and borrowing are not wrong.

c) Psalm 37:26

Here we see the commendation of a righteous man: "He is ever merciful, and lendeth; and his seed is blessed." The righteous are not only not forsaken (v. 25), but they are gracious and merciful enough to lend to others. Consequently, they are blessed. God blesses those who give out of their surplus to those in need.

d) Proverbs 19:7, 17

Proverbs 19:7 says, "All the brethren of the poor do hate him. How much more do his friends go far from him! He pursueth them with words, yet they are lacking to him." Sometimes poor people can't get what they need from the people who say they are their friends. Verse 17 adds, "He that hath pity upon the poor lendeth unto the Lord, and that which he hath given will he pay him again." When you lend money to someone who is in need, you are lending to the Lord. Therefore the issue is not whether the borrower pays you back; the Lord promises He will pay you back. I can give testimony from my own life that that's true. When my family has been asked to lend money to someone who was in great need of it, we did so in good faith with joyful and eager hearts. Never have we loaned someone money without experiencing the abundant blessing of God.

e) Matthew 5:42

Jesus said, "Give to him that asketh thee, and from him that would borrow of thee turn not thou away." When someone comes to you with a need, you should respond in eagerness to meet that need.

f) Luke 6:35

In this verse the Lord says, "Love ye your enemies, and do good, and lend, hoping for nothing again; and your reward shall be great."

2. Principles for loaning money

Both the Old and New Testaments indicate that the person who lends to others is generous. Lending is to be done in response to need, it should be done without interest, and it should be done with a willing heart. When you lend money, remember that it's as if you were lending to the Lord. He will give you an eternal and spiritual reward. Don't just focus on getting paid back. And interestingly, nowhere in the Bible is lending and borrowing talked about outside of the realm of needs. Scripture does not advocate going into debt for luxury. Someone has said, "Today, people buy things they don't need with money they don't have from people they don't even like."

In a parable in Matthew 25, the Lord said the servant who buried the one talent entrusted to him should have "put [the] money to the exchangers" so it would have received interest (v. 27). He was saying it's wise to invest money in the bank so it can earn interest. You give your money to the bank, who lends it out to others at some interest rate, and in turn the bank pays you interest. The Lord understood that sometimes businesses need to borrow money. Many businesses can't operate without borrowing, and most of us wouldn't be able to buy homes if we weren't allowed to take out loans.

Borrowing money is reasonable, particularly when it's done to meet the basic needs of life. It's like renting money, just as you rent a house or a car. However, keep this in mind: The borrower is servant to the lender (Prov. 22:7). Whatever money you owe to someone can't be used for anything else. Whatever money you owe toward paying a debt cannot be used by you or given to the Lord. So you want to be very careful about how much you borrow. And as Paul says in Romans 13:8, whatever you borrow must be paid back. The Bible doesn't forbid indebtedness, but it does forbid nonpayment of your debts. Psalm 37:21 says, "The wicked borroweth, and payeth not again." That is not acceptable to the Lord. Pay your debts. Owe no one anything that is overdue.

B. The Principle: Owing Love

After Paul said, "Owe no man any thing," he continued, "But to love one another" (Rom. 13:8). The only thing you'll always owe is love. Even though you constantly show love to others, you'll never pay off that debt. Origen, the third-century church Father, said that the debt of love remains with us permanently and never leaves us. It is a debt that we pay every day and forever owe. The apostle Paul was saying that love is something we owe to everyone in society. Our lives are to be marked by love.

1. The exhortation to love

   In John 13:35 Jesus says, "By this shall all men know that ye are my disciples, if ye have love one to another." First John 2:10 says, "He that loveth his brother abideth in the light." First John 3:23 says, "This is his commandment, that we should believe on the name of his Son, Jesus Christ, and love one another, as he gave us commandment." Later in the same epistle, we read, "Beloved, let us love one another; for love is of God. . . .And this commandment have we from him, that he who loveth God love his brother also" (4:7, 21).

   It is the mark of a Christian that he loves all people. We owe that debt to everyone. We pay it all our lives and never diminish it. We are called to love others. Jesus made that clear when He said this in Matthew 5:44-45: "Love your enemies, bless them that curse you, do good to them that hate you, and pray for them who despitefully use you, and persecute you, that ye may be the sons of your Father, who is in heaven." Since God loves those who are His enemies, you are to love them too. You are to be distinctively marked by love.

   Galatians 6:10 says, "Do good unto all men, especially unto them who are of the household of faith." In Colossians 3:14 Paul says, "Put on love." In Philippians 1:9 he says, "This I pray, that your love may abound." In 1 Timothy 2:15 we read, "Continue in . . . love," and 1 Peter 1:22, "Love one another with a pure heart fervently." We are to be bound together by love, "which is the bond of perfectness" (Col. 3:14). We are to love everyone; Christians ought to be known as those who love.

2. The elements of love

   What is love? How do you demonstrate it? Is it an emotion, a spiritual goose bump, or a warm, fuzzy feeling? When talking about love, it's important to look at what it is biblically.

   a) Love teaches others the truth of God

      In 2 Corinthians 6 Paul talks about all the things he is committed to, and what he had done for the Corinthians. For them he had been a servant of God "in stripes, in imprisonments, in tumults, in labors, in watchings, in fastings; by pureness, by knowledge, by long-suffering, by kindness, by the Holy Spirit, by love unfeigned, by the word of truth, by the power of God, by the armor of righteousness on the right hand and on the left" (vv. 5-7). The key is that he came to them by knowledge and the Word of truth. Love is a matter of articulating truth; it says what has to be said from God's Word. Ephesians 4:15 says we are to speak the truth in love. So love involves teaching others what needs to be taught. It is not a feeling, but an act.

b) Love ministers to the needs of others

One way you can show love to others is by helping them. Hebrews 6:10 says, "God is not unrighteous to forget your work and labor of love, which ye have shown toward his name, in that ye have ministered to the saints, and do minister." Your labor of love is your ministry to the needs of the saints. In that passage, love is a verb.

c) Love serves others and causes them to grow

Love sets a positive example of spiritual life that helps others to grow. To the Galatians Paul said, "Brethren, ye have been called unto liberty; only use not liberty for an occasion to the flesh, but by love serve one another" (Gal. 5:13). We have been called to liberty, but not to the extent that we offend others. Rather, we are to restrict our liberty to serve others. A loving person is cautious about his behavior and makes sure that it stimulates rather than retards the growth of others. Love serves others in a way that leads them to the Lord, not sin.

d) Love covers the sins of others

First Peter 4:8 says, "Love shall cover the multitude of sins." Love doesn't flaunt another person's faults.

Love teaches people the truth. If you love someone, you speak the truth and give him the Word of God. In 2 Corinthians 6:11-12 Paul says, "Our speech to you is candid, our heart is wide open. On our part there is no constraint, but there is constraint in your affections." Paul loved the Corinthians and was truthful with them, even though they loved him less for doing so. Second, love ministers to the needs of others. Third, it serves others with cautious behavior that leads people to the Lord and not sin. Love doesn't flaunt its liberty. And love covers faults; it does not hurry to expose other people's sins.

e) Love forgives

Ephesians 4:32—5:2 says, "Be ye kind one to another, tenderhearted, forgiving one another, even as God, for Christ's sake, hath forgiven you. Be ye, therefore, followers of God, as dear children; and walk in love, as Christ also hath loved us, and hath given himself for us." Just as Christ loved us and gave Himself for us, we are to love others and give ourselves for them. Love and forgive others as Christ did.

f) Love endures

First Corinthians 13:7 says that love "beareth all things, believeth all things, hopeth all things, endureth all things." Love endures; it is patient. In Ephesians 4:2 Paul says we are to forbear one another in love. We are to love others even when we know of their faults.

g) Love sacrifices for others

John 15:13-14 says, "Greater love hath no man than this, that a man lay down his life for his friends. Ye are my friends, if ye do whatever I command you."

Love is an action. It teaches the truth to others and ministers to their needs. It sets an example that doesn't lead people toward sin. It covers other people's faults and forgives. Love endures the problems and idiosyncrasies of others, and sacrifices in their behalf. Self-sacrificial love gives to those in need of spiritual truth, help, and concern; it's not an emotional love. We owe everyone that kind of love and should not owe anything else. Pay your debts and owe love. That's the heart of Christian living; it's the magnet that attracts the world.

3. The exercise of love

How is it possible for us to love like that? When a person becomes a Christian, God gives him a new capacity for love. Before you were saved, you couldn't love others in a self- sacrificing way, but now you can. Romans 5:5 says, "The love of God is shed abroad in our hearts by the Holy Spirit who is given unto us." We have within us a resource that enables us to love as we ought. We can love

100

as Epaphroditus did. He served Paul, the church, and the Lord so much that he almost died (Phil. 2:25-27). God lavishly pours out His love to us, and that becomes the well we draw from when we show love to others.

We're supposed to be obedient. One way we can be obedient is by loving everyone. The only way we can do that is by having a supernatural love, which comes only from God. That becomes the well we draw from. How can we lower our spiritual buckets into that well to draw from that love? How do we appropriate what God has given us? Let's see how we can do that.

a) Understand the resource

You have the capacity to love others. In Ephesians 3:18-19 Paul prays that we "may be able to comprehend, with all saints, what is the breadth, and length, and depth, and height, and to know the love of Christ, which passeth knowledge." You need to comprehend what's available to you. God has enabled you to love everyone in every possible situation. The well is more than sufficient. Seize that resource, and make it your own by faith. You need to acknowledge that you have the resource within you to love those around you.

b) Submit to the Holy Spirit

You need to learn to give the Holy Spirit complete control over your life. You can either hold onto your feelings of bitterness, anxiety, and hatred toward someone, or you can yield them to the Spirit of God. When you submit to the Holy Spirit, He takes over your life and replaces bitterness with love and vengeance with affection. In 1 Thessalonians 4:9 Paul says, "As touching brotherly love, ye need not that I write unto you; for ye yourselves are taught of God to love one another." How is that possible? The Spirit of God has shed that love abroad in our hearts (Rom. 5:5). In Galatians 5:22 love is mentioned as a part of the fruit of the Spirit.

The capacity to love everyone is available within us; we must understand the resource. If you submit to the Holy Spirit, He will teach you how to love. You are taught of God to love one another. You don't need to be taught by someone else how to do that.

101

c) Purify your heart

In 1 Peter 1:22 we read these words: "Seeing that ye have purified your souls in obeying the truth through the Spirit unto unfeigned love of the brethren, see that ye love one another with a pure heart fervently." Before you can love others as you should, you must have a pure heart. You won't be able to show true love for others until you've dealt with the sin in your life. You must recognize as sin any bitterness, vengeance, and hostility in your life. You must confess and deal with any wrong attitude in your life.

d) Possess a sense of urgency

First Peter 4:7 says, "The end of all things is at hand; be ye, therefore, sober-minded, and watch unto prayer. And above all things have fervent love among yourselves; for love shall cover the multitude of sins." One key reason we are to love others is that the end of all things is at hand. We need to sense the urgency to love others and live the way we ought to live. We need to let our lives attract people to the Lord.

e) Consciously choose to love others

In Colossians 3:14 we read, "Above all these things put on love." We should make a conscious choice to love others. Some time ago I counseled a couple who had been struggling seriously in their marriage for quite a while. I shared with them that they needed to make a conscious choice to love each other. They had to train themselves to love at times when they felt angry or taken advantage of. They needed to replace rudeness and unkind words with love. Two days after our talk, the husband called me and said, "I just wanted to let you know that each time a problem arises, we are endeavoring to do all we can in the Spirit of God to make a conscious choice to love, make peace, and show kindness no matter what the price to our own ego might be." Choosing to love and forgive others is a factor in learning how to pay the debt of love. The Spirit of God enables you to do that when you train your mind and make a commitment to obey the Lord.

f) Interact with other believers

You'll find it difficult to love others when you are isolated. Hebrews 10:24-25 says, "Let us consider one another to provoke unto love and to good works, not forsaking the assembling of ourselves together, as the manner of some is, but exhorting one another, and so much the more, as ye see the day approaching." The dynamics of Christian fellowship help us to love and be accountable to one another.

g) Concentrate on others

In Philippians 2 Paul says, "If there be, therefore, any consolation in Christ, if any comfort of love, if any fellowship of the Spirit, if any tender mercies an compassions, fulfill ye my joy, that ye be like-minded, having the same love, being of one accord, of one mind. Let nothing be done through strife or vainglory, but in lowliness of mind let each esteem others better than themselves" (vv. 1-3). If there is going to be love in the fellowship, we have to be preoccupied with others. I shouldn't be looking for people to love me; I should be looking for ways to love others.

h) Consider the results

Loving others brings wonderful results. Let's look at the life of our Lord Himself: Scripture indicates that He loved, and as a result of His love He was loved in return (1 John 4:19). There's a dynamic in love that is reciprocal. People want to be loved. If we focus on loving others, we will be loved!

We are to love others; that's a debt we have to pay. How do we pay it? By understanding our resource. Love is available to us, and it's our fault if we don't tap the necessary resource. We are to submit to the Spirit and learn how to love. We must purify our hearts by confessing our sin and realizing the urgency of attracting others to Christ through our love. We are to make a conscious choice to love others, fellowship with other believers, and concentrate on others rather than ourselves. And we must consider the effect of loving others. Love given is inevitably love returned.

When God saved us, we were made a new creation with the capacity to fulfill the debt of love. The reservoir of love is inexhaustible. We have the privilege of representing God in the world by loving others as He loved them and receiving love in return.

Someone has written, "By its very nature, love is the duty which when done, is never done, since he loves not truly who loves for the purpose of ceasing to love. . . .By loving, love is intensified—the more it is exercised, the less it can become satisfied." Love, then, should be the desire of the regenerate heart. In fact, it is the supreme aspect of our obedience. And we can fulfill the debt of love because of the new capacity God has given us.

A Homework Assignment on Love

You say, "I want to pay the debt of love that I owe. What should I do?" Here are some suggestions:

- Mend a quarrel.
- Call a friend you haven't seen for a long time.
- Replace a suspicion with trust.
- Remove any bitterness in your life.
- Write a surprise letter to someone who loves you.
- Tell someone you know well how much he means to you.
- Keep a promise.
- Ask God to forgive someone who did something wrong to you, and forget the wrongdoing.
- Don't be overly demanding on the other members of your family.
- Express thanks to others throughout the day.
- Tell someone you love that you care about him.
- Pray for one of your enemies.
- Send a check to someone who has a need.

Ask God to help you love the way Jesus loved!

Focusing on the Facts

1. What is one key distinction between a true Christian and someone who merely professes to be a Christian (see p. 92)?
2. Explain how we can still be bound to the law, even though we are saved by grace (see p. 92).
3. What is the key to obedience? How can we overcome the flesh's desire to disobey? Explain (see p. 93).
4. What do the results of our salvation include (Rom. 12-13; see pp. 93-94)?
5. In Romans 13:8 Paul says, "Owe no man any thing." Explain the transition Paul was making from verses 6-7 to verse 8 (see p. 94).

6. Discuss what Scripture says about borrowing money (see pp. 94-96).
7. Summarize the basic principles for loaning money (see pp. 96-97).
8. For what does Scripture advocate borrowing money (see p. 97)?
9. How will unsaved people know we belong to Christ (John 13:35)? What exhortation are we given in 1 John 4:7 and 21 (see p. 98)?
10. What does love teach? To what does love minister (see pp. 98-99)?
11. In what way should we serve others (see p. 99)?
12. To what extent are we to forgive others (Eph. 4:32—5:2; see p. 100)?
13. What does John 15:13-14 say about love (see p. 100)?
14. How is it possible for us to love in a self-sacrificial manner (Rom. 5:5; see pp. 100-101)?
15. How does the Holy Spirit help us to overcome our bad attitudes (see p. 101)?
16. What must you have before you can love others (1 Pet. 1:22; see p. 102)?
17. What does Colossians 3:14 tell us to do? Explain (see p. 102).
18. What important application can we make from Philippians 2:1-3 (see p. 103)?
19. Mention several ways we can pay the debt of love (see p. 104).

Pondering the Principles

1. Matthew 5:42 says, "Give to him that asketh thee, and from him that would borrow of thee turn not thou away." Think of different kinds of needs people have and write them down. Next to each need, write how that need can be met. One observation you might make from your list is that needs aren't always financial; there are also spiritual needs that require a listening ear, a word of encouragement, or some counsel from the Bible. Think of a Christian or a non-Christian you know who has a need you can meet, and satisfy that need this week. Ask God to help you be sensitive to the needs of others, and to be preoccupied with others and not yourself.

2. It's important for us to remember our debt of love. Memorize Romans 13:8 to help you do that: "Let no debt remain outstanding, except the continuing debt to love one another, for he who loves his fellow man has fulfilled the law" (NIV).

3. Reread the section entitled "The elements of love," on pages 98-100. Spend some time thinking about how you can apply the elements you need to work on and how you can encourage other

Christians to develop those that you are already actively applying. What can you learn from the example of other Christians who are exhibiting these elements toward you?

7

Love Fulfills the Law—
Part 2

Outline

Introduction

Review
I. The Debt of Love

Lesson
II. The Discharge to Love
   A. The Statement
   B. The Specifics
   C. The Source
   D. The Statutes
      1. Concerning our relationship with God
        a) Love is loyal
        b) Love is faithful
        c) Love is reverent
        d) Love is holy
      2. Concerning our relationships with others
        a) Love is respectful
        b) Love is protective
        c) Love is pure
        d) Love is unselfish
        e) Love is truthful
        f) Love is content
   E. The Summation
III. The Design of Love
   A. Failing the Law
   B. Fulfilling the Law
      1. The principles
      2. The practice

Conclusion

Introduction

In Romans 13:8-10 Paul writes, "Owe no man any thing, but to love one another; for he that loveth another hath fulfilled the law. For this, Thou shalt not commit adultery, Thou shalt not kill, Thou shalt not steal, Thou shalt not bear false witness, Thou shalt not covet; and if there by any other commandment, it is briefly comprehended in this saying, namely, Thou shalt love thy neighbor as thyself. Love worketh no ill to its neighbor; therefore, love is the fulfilling of the law."

Review

In our last lesson, we learned that one of the results of salvation and being made right with God is a new and unique relationship to society: a relationship of love. Jesus says in John 13:34, "A new commandment I give unto you, that ye love one another; as I have loved you, that ye also love one another." The distinguishing mark of a Christian is love. Love fulfills the law, as the apostle Paul says in Romans 13:8-10. He discussed three features of love in that passage: the debt of love, the discharge to love, and the design of love.

I. THE DEBT OF LOVE (v. 8*a*; see pp. 94-104)

Lesson

II. THE DISCHARGE TO LOVE (vv. 9-10*a*)

    A. The Statement

        In Romans 13:9-10, Paul shows how the new law is "the royal law" of love (James 2:8). He says the law of love is an all-encompassing law in Romans 13:9-10: "Thou shalt not commit adultery, Thou shalt not kill, Thou shalt not steal, Thou shalt not bear false witness, Thou shalt not covet; and if there be any other commandment, it is briefly comprehended in this saying, namely, Thou shalt love thy neighbor as thyself. Love worketh no ill to its neighbor."

        Romans 13:9 is a summation of the law of God. The apostle said the law of love fulfills all other laws. The Ten Commandments are all fulfilled in the royal law, which is the law of love. Paul shows us in Romans 13 that love and the law are not contradictory. They are not mutually exclusive; rather, love is the fulfilling of the law. The Ten Commandments can be summarized in two statements: "Thou shalt love the Lord, thy God, with all thy heart, and with all thy soul, and with all thy mind. This is the first and great commandment" (Matt. 22:37-38), and, "Thou shalt love thy neighbor as thyself" (v. 39). The Lord said that "on these two commandments hang all the law and the prophets" (v. 40). Paul makes the same point in Romans 13:9-10. If we who are Christians ask, "How can I fulfill the law of God?" the answer is, "By loving God and others." Love is the fulfillment of the law.

B. The Specifics

To illustrate his point in Romans 13:9, Paul selects four of the Ten Commandments: the seventh, the sixth, the eighth, and the tenth. Commandments five through ten make up the second section of the commandments, those that deal with our relationships with others. I don't think Paul left out the fifth and ninth Commandments for any particular reason; he simply chose the others as a sampling. After he stated the four commandments, notice that he covered the missing commandments by saying, "If there be any other commandment" (Rom. 13:9).

The four commandments Paul cited are not in the same sequence as they are in the Hebrew text; they are in the same order as they appear in the Septuagint (the Greek version of the Old Testament) in Deuteronomy 5:17-21. He simply listed four of the commandments and said, "If you know these things, you know the whole law. And the law is summed up in this statement: Love your neighbor as you love yourself." The whole law is encompassed in that one statement; the key to obeying the law is love.

When we love others, we will automatically obey the law. You don't need to worry about committing adultery if you love someone. Some couples say, "We committed adultery because we loved each other too much." My answer to that is, "No, you committed adultery because you love each other too little." Love doesn't defile others or steal purity. Only lust and selfishness do that. A person will never commit adultery or fornication because he loves too much.

If you love someone, your love renders useless the command not to kill. I don't need someone to remind me not to kill people if I love them. When you love someone, you won't steal from him. Therefore, it's unnecessary to say, "Thou shalt not steal." Nor will you covet what someone else has when you love him. So love doesn't replace the law; it fulfills the law. Through love, God's whole law can be fulfilled.

C. The Source

Since love fulfills the law, we know God does not want just outward obedience. The Pharisees used to say, "We don't commit adultery, kill people, steal from people, or covet things." But in their hearts, they did. They committed adultery in their minds, they were murderous in their thoughts, they stole intangibly, and they coveted what they didn't have. They lived by an external law with an external definition that they could fulfill. But Scripture says you are to love so that you don't commit adultery. It doesn't say to avoid committing adultery out of fear of getting caught or so that you can appear pious. Your motive for not killing others should be your love for them.

The keeping of a commandment should flow from a heart of love. It's possible to obey the law out of fear and to be afraid of God's punishment. But when you do that, you don't really obey the law in the fullest sense because fear is not the biblical motive for obedience. The Bible doesn't say, "You shall dread the Lord your God with all your heart, soul, mind, and strength." Isaiah 29:13 says that many people draw near to God with their lips, but their hearts are far from Him. Fear will restrain you from some evil and its effect can be somewhat productive, but it is incomplete. We are to keep the law not out of fear only but also out of love.

There are some people who keep the law out of self-interest. There are people who believe that if they live a moral life, God will repay them. But that is not a pure motive for obedience; it's a selfish one. Although you may restrain yourself from evil and do good things outwardly, you won't have an obedience that comes from an attitude of love. The true intention of the law is to cultivate love from the heart. That's how the law is fulfilled. In Matthew 22 Jesus says, "Thou shalt love the Lord, thy God, with all thy heart, and with all thy soul, and with all thy mind. This is the first and great commandment. And the second is like it, Thou shalt love thy neighbor as thyself. On these two commandments hang all the law and the prophets" (vv. 37-40).

D. The Statutes

Let's take a look at the Ten Commandments in Exodus 20, and see how they could be considered the law of love. The first four commandments talk about our relationship with God, and the last six deal with our relationships with men.

1. Concerning our relationship with God

    a) Love is loyal

    In Exodus 20:3 God says, "Thou shalt have no other
    gods before me." That's a perfect description of love:
    It is loyal. Love is true and single-minded, not fickle.
    If you truly love God, you will not show love toward
    any other deity. If you really love God, you'll be loyal
    to Him.

    b) Love is faithful

    Exodus 20:4-6 says, "Thou shalt not make unto thee
    any carved image, or any likeness of anything that is
    in heaven above, or that is in the earth beneath, or
    that is in the water under the earth; thou shalt not
    bow down thyself to them, nor serve them; for I, the
    Lord thy God, am a jealous God, visiting the iniquity
    of the fathers upon the children unto the third and
    fourth generation of them that hate me; and showing
    mercy unto thousands of them that love me and keep
    my commandments." Love is faithful; it is devoted to
    its object, and it obeys.

    c) Love is reverent

    In Exodus 20:7 we read, "Thou shalt not take the
    name of the Lord thy God in vain; for the Lord will
    not hold him guiltless that taketh his name in vain."

    If you love God, will you curse His name? If you love
    Him, will you be unfaithful to His Word or be disloyal
    to Him and follow another deity? Of course not!
    Reverence, faithfulness, and loyalty are ways of dem-
    onstrating love.

    d) Love is holy

    Exodus 20:8-11 says, "Remember the sabbath day, to
    keep it holy. Six days shalt thou labor and do all thy
    work; but the seventh day is the sabbath of the Lord
    thy God; in it thou shalt not do any work, thou, nor
    thy son, nor thy daughter, thy manservant, nor thy
    maidservant, nor thy cattle, nor thy stranger that is
    within thy gates; for in six days the Lord made
    heaven and earth, the sea, and all that in them is, and
    rested the seventh day; wherefore, the Lord blessed
    the sabbath day, and hallowed it." Love sets apart

itself for pure, uncompromising devotion. Love recognizes the priority of worship.

If you love God, you will worship Him. If you say you love God, you will serve Him and keep His commandments. You will be faithful to His Word, reverent to His name, and loyal to Him as your only God. The first four of the Ten Commandments sum up the first and great commandment of Deuteronomy 6, which is quoted by Christ in Matthew 22: "Thou shalt love the Lord thy God with all thine heart, and with all thy soul, and with all thy might" (Deut. 6:5). If I love the Lord that way, will I have to worry about trying to keep the first four commandments? No, because if I really love Him, I will never have any other god or make a graven image. I will always obey Him, never take His name in vain, and remember to worship Him. Thus, love fulfills the law.

2. Concerning our relationships with others

The commandments Paul cites in Romans 13:9 come from this section of the Ten Commandments.

a) Love is respectful

Exodus 20:12 says, "Honor thy father and thy mother, that thy days may be long upon the land which the Lord thy God giveth thee." If you love your father and mother, you will honor them. Love is respectful; it bows to authority. It respects those who are worthy of respect.

b) Love is protective

In Exodus 20:13 we read, "Thou shalt not kill." Love doesn't slaughter other people; it protects them. It believes every life is sacred, and that everyone is created in the image of God.

c) Love is pure

We read in Exodus 20:14, "Thou shalt not commit adultery." Love doesn't defile other people. Love lives to exalt what is holy, good, and virtuous.

d) Love is unselfish

Exodus 20:15 says, "Thou shalt not steal." Love doesn't take something that belongs to someone else. It gives rather than takes.

e) Love is truthful

In Exodus 20:16 we read, "Thou shalt not bear false witness against thy neighbor." Love doesn't lie; it doesn't give false testimony.

f) Love is content

Exodus 20:17 says, "Thou shalt not covet thy neighbor's house; thou shalt not covet thy neighbor's wife, nor his manservant, nor his maidservant, nor his ox, nor his ass, nor anything that is thy neighbor's."

Love fulfills the whole law. The last six commandments fulfill the second great commandment, which is, "Thou shalt love thy neighbor as thyself" (Matt. 22:39). That's what Paul talks about in Romans 13:9: fulfilling the law by love. He said, "Thou shalt not commit adultery, Thou shalt not kill, Thou shalt not steal, Thou shalt not bear false witness, Thou shalt not covet; and if there be any other commandment, it is briefly comprehended in this saying, namely, Thou shalt love thy neighbor as thyself" (v. 9). The saying at the end of the verse is an exact quote from Leviticus 19:18.

E. The Summation

What is God saying in the Ten Commandments? He sums up the whole law in two commands: "Love Me, and love men." Christ said that on those two commandments "hang all the law and the prophets" (Matt. 22:40). Sometimes you might look at a big, thick Bible and wonder, "How can I know and keep all the rules in God's Word?" It's very simple: Love God, love men, and do what you want. You say, "You're kidding!" No. When you love God with all your heart, soul, mind, and strength, and you love your neighbor as yourself, you can do what you want because you will be exactly what God wants you to be. Because of your love, you won't kill anyone, defile anyone, steal anything, or covet what another person has. The Spirit of God cultivates in the believer's heart a love that precludes any desire to do wrong.

Do unto Others as You Do unto Yourself

What did Paul mean when he said, "Love thy neighbor as thyself" (Rom. 13:9)? He was not talking about some kind of psychological self-love or developing a healthy self-image. He was saying, "You take care of yourself more than you take care of anyone else, and should have the same concern for others that you have for yourself." Paul made a similar statement in Philippians 2:4: "Look not every man on his own things, but every man also on the things of others." You should be just as concerned about the comfort, happiness, peace, and joy of others as you are about your own. Whose face do you wash in the morning? Whose hair do you comb? Whose wardrobe do you buy? Whose comforts are you concerned about? You are concerned about your self-preservation and self-comfort and should be concerned about others in the same way. Pay as much attention to them as you do yourself. That's loving your neighbor as yourself.

Who is your neighbor? Anyone who comes across your path. Although it's hard to love everyone, you have a new capacity within you to do that: The love of Christ is shed abroad in your heart (Rom. 5:5). If you want to know how love acts, read 1 Corinthians 13.

The debt of love is unpayable. You will pay it all your life and never pay it off. That debt is to keep on loving others. You are to show love to everyone. When you love that way, you will fulfill the law. You will never harm a person you love.

III. THE DESIGN OF LOVE (vv. 8b, 10b)

Paul wrote, "He that loveth another hath fulfilled the law. . . . Therefore, love is the fulfilling of the law" (vv. 8, 10). Romans 13:8 literally says, "The one loving has fulfilled the other law." Paul was referring to the second greatest commandment in Matthew 22:39: "Thou shalt love thy neighbor as thyself." One who loves others fulfills the second greatest law. Romans 13:10 states that love is the fulfilling of the law; it gives to the law the full measure of its fulfillment.

A. Failing the Law

A Pharisee or a legalist—someone who keeps the law out of fear or self-interest—can never really fulfill the law. You can restrain yourself from committing adultery, murdering, lying, or coveting the things of others out of fear or a legalistic desire to appear pious, but you won't fulfill the law by doing that. The only way to fulfill the law is by having a love for God and others that comes from within you. Such love can be a reality because of the work of Jesus Christ.

B. Fulfilling the Law

In Matthew 5:17 we read that Jesus came not to destroy the law, but to fulfill it. He fulfilled it in terms of prophecy, He fulfilled it by keeping it perfectly, and He fulfilled it by being the perfect expression of love. In every way that the law could be fulfilled, He fulfilled it.

1. The principles

God has called us to love. When we do that, we fulfill the whole law. We are to love everyone in society; Paul tells us that beginning in Romans 12. From chapter 3 to 11, he talks about redemption. Then from chapter 12 on, Paul talks about the results of our redemption. First, we are to present our bodies to God (12:1). We are no longer conformed to this world (v. 2). We are to use our spiritual gifts (vv. 3-8), and demonstrate certain virtues and grace to the church and the world around us (vv. 9-21). We are to submit ourselves to the government and pay our taxes (13:1-7). And in our relationships to everyone, we are to be characterized by love (vv. 8-10). We are told in John 13:34-35, "A new commandment I give unto you, that ye love one another; as I have loved you. . . . By this shall all men know that ye are my disciples." Love fulfills the law. It is a comprehensive grace that includes all aspects of Christian living, attitude, speech, and action. The only way you can fulfill the law is through love, and you should love everyone around you.

2. The practice

First Corinthians 13 makes practical the concept of loving one another. Here is an interesting paraphrase of verses 1-3: "If I have the language perfectly and speak like a native, and have not His love for them, I am nothing. If I have diplomas and degrees and know all the up-to-date methods, and have not His touch of understanding love, I am nothing. If I am able to argue successfully against the religions of the people and make fools of them, and have not His wooing note, I am nothing. If I have all faith and great ideals and magnificent plans, and not His love that sweats and bleeds and weeps and prays and pleads, I am nothing. If I give my clothes and money to them, and have not His love for them, I am nothing.

"If I surrender all prospects, leave home and friends, make the sacrifices of a missionary career, and turn sour and selfish amid the daily annoyances and slights of a missionary life, and have not the love that yields its rights, its leisures, its pet plans, I am nothing. Virtue has ceased to go out of me. If I can heal all manner of sickness and disease, but wound hearts and hurt feelings for want of His love that is kind, I am nothing. If I can write articles or publish books that win applause, but fail to transcribe the Word of the Cross into the language of His love, I am nothing" (Paul Lee Tan, *Encyclopedia of 7700 Illustrations* [Rockville, Maryland: Assurance Publishers, 1979], pp. 758-59).

Conclusion

We owe a debt to love. It's possible to love as we should because the Lord has given us the capacity to do so. We have been given a new command to love one another (John 13:34-35). The design of love is that we fulfill the law of God. What could never be done through the law can be done through the love we receive when we are saved. Believers are to be marked by love. The world is watching us, and so is the Lord. What they both wish to see is love in the little things as well as the big things.

Focusing on the Facts

1. What does Romans 13:9 summarize (see p. 108)?
2. How did Paul compensate for not mentioning all the commandments in Romans 13:9 (see p. 109)?
3. When we love others, what will automatically happen? Explain (see p. 110).
4. What should be your motive for keeping the commandments? What is wrong with keeping the commandments with motives other than that (see p. 110)?
5. With what do the first four commandments deal? What about the last six commandments (see p. 110)?
6. How should we show our love for God (see pp. 111-112)?
7. How should we show our love for other people (see pp. 112-113)?
8. In what two commands does God sum up the whole law (see p. 113)?
9. Discuss the significance of the phrase "love thy neighbor as thyself" (Rom. 13:9). Who is your neighbor (see pp. 113-114)?
10. How did Christ fulfill the law (see pp. 114-115)?
11. The only way you can fulfill the —————— is through —————— (see p. 115).

Pondering the Principles

1. Take some time to think about some ways you have helped others in the past few weeks. Would God be pleased with the motives you had in each of the instances that come to your mind? Have

116

you recently helped others with the hope of receiving something in return? Everything you do for another person should be done out of love for that person and for God. What are some ways you can keep your motives pure?

2. What do these verses tell us about loving others: 2 Corinthians 8:8, Philippians 1:9, and Hebrews 10:24? What are some different ways we can put each of those exhortations into practice? What would be some of the results of demonstrating love in those ways?

8

The Humility of Love

Outline

Introduction
A. Christ's Selflessness
B. Christ's Service

Lesson
I. The Statement of Christ's Love (v. 1)
   A. Explaining the Extent of Christ's Love
   B. Exemplifying the Extent of Christ's Love (v. 2)
II. The Spurning of Christ's Love
   A. Judas's Hatred
   B. Jesus' Love
III. The Showing of Christ's Love (vv. 3-11)
   A. The Exaltation of Christ (v.3)
   B. The Humiliation of Christ (vv. 4-11)
     1. The details
     2. The display
     3. The dialogue
       a) The first exchange
       b) The second exchange
     4. The declaration
       a) The requirement for spiritual cleansing
       b) The rejection of spiritual cleansing
IV. The Sharing of Christ's Love (vv. 12-17)
   A. The Inquiry (v. 12)
   B. The Instruction (vv. 13-17)
     1. The request for humility (vv. 13-15)
     2. The result of humility (vv. 16-17)

Conclusion

Introduction

In John 13 there is a great example of the humility of love. The greatest virtue of love is its humility, for that's what measures love and makes it serviceable. The picture of love in John 13 is one of the most beautiful in Scripture. The apostle Paul said that love doesn't seek its own (1 Cor. 13:5). It is not selfish; rather, it always gives. Love is always humble. In John 13 we will see the unselfish quality of true love, and study what believers through the ages have regarded as one of the most precious portions in all the New Testament.

John 13 begins a new section in the gospel of John, the previous section ending at chapter 12. In John 1-12, we read about the rejection of Christ by the nation of Israel and in chapters 13-17, we have the record of those who received Him. It was those who put their faith in Him who became children of God (John 1:12). John 12:36 tells us that when the public ministry of Jesus ended: "These things spoke Jesus, and [He] departed, and did hide himself from them." Christ had presented Himself to Israel—they had seen His miracles, heard His words, and observed His love—yet they concluded that He was empowered by Satan (Matt. 12:24). They totally rejected Christ and fulfilled the words of John 1:11: "He came unto his own, and his own received him not."

From John 13 onward, Christ moves completely away from His public ministry to His private ministry with those who did receive Him. The Lord's call to Israel had run its course. He no longer showed His grace to Israel; instead, He spent time in intimate fellowship with His disciples. In John 13-17 the key thing He reveals in that fellowship is His love for them.

William Barclay summarizes well what happens in John 13: "Jesus knew that all things had been given into His hands. He knew that His hour of humiliation was near, but He knew also that His hour of glory was near. He knew that it was not long now until He took His place upon the very throne of God. Such a thought and such a consciousness might well have filled Him with pride; and yet, with the knowledge of the power and the glory that were His, He washed His disciples' feet" (*The Gospel of John*, vol. 2 [Philadelphia: Westminster, 1956], p. 159).

A. Christ's Selflessness

Thoughts about the cross, death, the resurrection, the ascension, and His glorification at the right hand of the Father must have crowded our Lord's brain on the day before His death. It would have been easy for Him to be preoccupied with Himself. Christ could have easily thought He should be proud of Himself because He would soon bear the sins of the world, rise out of the grave, ascend into heaven, and be exalted at the right hand of the Father. He knew of the glory that awaited Him, and that every knee would bow before Him (Phil. 2:9-11). But instead of being proud of Himself, He stooped over to do what was perhaps the second most humiliating thing in His life beside His death: He washed the feet of His disciples. William Barclay said of Jesus, "Just at that moment when He might have had the supreme pride, He had the supreme humility" (*The Gospel of John*, vol. 2, p. 159).

B. Christ's Service

Just when Jesus could have exalted Himself and gloried in what was about to happen, He reached the depths of humility. Love does that. Loveless people feel too important to do menial tasks. But Christ wasn't that way. Even though He was fully conscious that He was the Lord of the universe, the King of kings and Lord of lords, God incarnate, He still washed the disciples' feet. That's the character of love; it is selfless.

In Christ's time, washing the feet of a man or a woman was the duty of a slave. The disciples of the Jewish rabbis normally rendered most personal services to their masters, but even they were to get a slave when the rabbi's feet needed washing. To wash another person's feet was considered the bottom rung on the ladder of service. The wonderful thing about Jesus' ministry was that He served sinners in the humblest ways. Some people think that the nearer you are to God, the further you become from men. But that's not true. The nearer you are to God, the closer you are to the hearts of men. Someone once said, "Some people are so heavenly minded, they're no earthly good." Such people have a false kind of service and a false nearness to God. True proximity to God involves serving someone else.

When the disciples were aware that Christ's ministry on earth was coming to an end, they may have thought His love for them would end with it. They were probably feeling despondent and lonely. Jesus wanted to dispel their fears and reassure them that His love is everlasting. In John 13-17 He does everything possible to show that. In John 13 He washes the disciples' feet. In chapter 14-16 He gives them a farewell address that shows His love. Then in chapter 17 He prays His high-priestly prayer on their behalf. Beyond that, the most supreme display of His love for them was His death on the cross. Christ did all He could to show the disciples that He loved them, and would continue to love them always. Love is the motive for everything that happens in John 13-17. You could say that that section of Scripture is the revelation of Christ's tender love for His own. How precious it is that Jesus shows such love for us in those passages!

On the day before His death, Christ wasn't preoccupied with His death and glorification. Rather, He was totally consumed with His love for the disciples. Even while keeping the task of redeeming the world in mind, He was preoccupied showing His love to the twelve. That's the mystery of Christ's love. He showed His love for the disciples in the greatest way possible—through humility. That's how love is made visible. In this study, there are four things we will look at: the statement of Christ's love, the spurning of Christ's love, the showing of Christ's love, and the sharing of Christ's love.

Lesson

I. THE STATEMENT OF CHRIST'S LOVE (v. 1)

"Now before the feast of the passover, when Jesus knew that his hour was come that he should depart out of this world unto the Father, having loved his own who were in the world, he loved them unto the end."

One commentator said it's very easy to interpret that verse: "Before the feast of the Passover, Jesus loved them, and He loved them until the end of the feast of the Passover." That's ridiculous! Christ didn't just love His disciples from the beginning of the Passover to the end of it. We'll see that when we examine the phrase "unto the end" a little later in the text.

Setting the Stage for a Transition

On Friday, Jesus was to die as the true Passover lamb. In Israel, all the pilgrims had arrived in Jerusalem to prepare themselves for the Passover. After that, there would be the seven-day feast of unleavened bread, which was a part of the Passover. The Passover was the annual Hebrew festival held on the fourteenth of Nisan, commemorating what God had done when the Israelites were in Egypt. Before the Israelites were allowed to leave Egypt, God brought ten plagues to the land to make the Pharaoh let them go. Prior to the last plague, during which all the firstborn

121

in the land of Egypt died, God said to the Israelites that He would send an angel of death over the land to kill the firstborn of every living thing. But He said if they sprinkled blood on the doorposts and lintels of their houses, the angel would pass over them and their firstborn would not die (Ex. 12:12-13). Every year after that the Jews celebrated Passover, remembering the protection of God when He killed all the firstborn in Egypt and passed over every home that had blood sprinkled on the doorframe. That's a picture of Christ, the true Passover lamb.

During the Passover, many Jews were gathered in Jerusalem. As far as God was concerned, it was the last significant Passover. From that point on, there would be a new supper: not the Passover feast, but the Lord's Supper. God's people would no longer commemorate the lambs' blood on the doorposts, but the Lamb of God slain on the cross once and forever. This was to be the last Passover. The other gospels tell us that before the Passover meal of John 13 was over, Jesus had already instituted the Lord's Supper. So this was a time of great transition—from the Passover of the Old Testament to the Lord's Supper of the New Testament. The New Testament age was beginning. No longer would men remember Passover lambs in Egypt, but the slain lamb Jesus Christ. And that remembrance wouldn't be just once a year, but all the time.

John 13:1 tells us, "Jesus knew that his hour was come that he should depart out of this world unto the Father." Christ was on a divine time schedule, and He knew it. As we learned earlier, it would have been very easy for Him to become preoccupied with His glorification. Instead, He focused on showing His love for the disciples. We know that He was looking forward to what was to come, because in John 17:5 He says, "Father, glorify thou me with thine own self with the glory which I had with thee before the world was." Christ wanted to return to glory; He longed to be in God's presence again. Yet He was concerned with revealing His love to the twelve that they might be secure.

A. Explaining the Extent of Christ's Love

John 13:1 says, "Having loved his own who were in the world, [Christ] loved them unto the end." What is meant by the phrase "he loved them unto the end"? That's the key to understanding John 13:1. The phrase "unto the end" in the Greek text is *eis telos*. John was saying that Jesus loved the disciples to perfection. He loved them to the uttermost with the fullness of His love. With a knowledge of His coming death, resurrection, and glorification, He was still preoccupied with showing perfect, consuming love for His disciples. All the way to the cross, through the grave, and on into eternity He loved them completely. The Greek text could not have used a better word to indicate the extent of Christ's love. The Lord loved His disciples to the furthest degree possible.

B. Exemplifying the Extent of Christ's Love

You might think that the disciples didn't deserve such love. That's right, but that's not the point. It's Christ's nature to love completely. When He was arrested, He protected the disciples from being arrested (John 18:8). While on the cross, He took care of His mother Mary by having John take her into his home (John 19:26-27). He gathered the dying thief next to Him into His arms (in a spiritual sense) and saved him (Luke 23:42-43). Even in the last hours of bearing the sins of the world, He was conscious of the one would-be disciple hanging next to Him. Jesus always focused on loving others to the uttermost. Someone wrote,

> His love no end or measure knows,
> No change can turn its course;
> Eternally the same it flows
> From one eternal source.

The Lord loves His own. In "I Am His and He Is Mine," one of my favorite hymns, nineteenth-century hymnwriter Wade Robinson wrote these words:

> Loved with everlasting love,
> Led by grace that love to know—
> Spirit, breathing from above,
> Thou hast taught me it is so!
> Of this full and perfect peace,
> O this transport all divine—
> In a love which cannot cease,
> I am His and He is mine.

Seeing the love Jesus Christ had for His own gives us insight into the character of divine love. Christ's love for His own was like that of a mother on her deathbed who loses herself in her love for her children even when she's breathing the last breath of life. In the last moments of His life before He went to the cross, Christ poured out His love for the twelve men gathered around Him. He

123

loved them completely, without reservation. Only absolute humility can generate such absolute love.

II. THE SPURNING OF CHRIST'S LOVE (v. 2)

"And, supper being ended, the devil having now put into the heart of Judas Iscariot [i.e., Judas, from the town of Karioth], Simon's son, to betray him."

A. Judas's Hatred

The phrase "supper being ended" is not an accurate renditon of the Greek text. A more accurate reading discovered in recent years is "the supper having begun," or "the supper being in progress." While the supper was in progress, the devil moved into the heart of Judas to influence him to betray Christ. Although the devil had been working in Judas to some degree before the supper, the Holy Spirit says what He does in verse 2 to provide a contrast to the love Christ was showering on the disciples. In the midst of Christ's total love, we see absolute hatred in Judas. It's hard to imagine how anyone could reject that kind of love. He did, and men still do today. The tragedy of Judas is that he constantly basked in the light while living in darkness. He felt the love of Christ, yet hated Him at the same time.

B. Jesus' Love

The Holy Spirit gives a tremendous contrast between Jesus and Judas in John 13:2. It's hard to define Christ's love, so the Spirit defines it by contrast. The apostle Paul had a hard time defining Christ's love, and so did John. In 1 John 3:1 the latter says, "Behold, what manner of love the Father hath bestowed upon us." He could have said, "Behold, what fantastic, stupendous, monumental love." He was probably at a loss for words and just wrote, "Behold, what manner of love." In Ephesians 2:4 Paul writes, "God . . . is rich in mercy, for his great love with which he loved us." In John 13:2 the magnitude of Christ's love is described without words and is contrasted with the blackest kind of hatred and rejection, which makes Christ's love look all the more glorious.

The astounding thing about Jesus is that the more men hated Him, the more He loved them. When someone hates you, it's easy to be bitter and resentful toward that person. But Christ wasn't that way. He responded to the greatest injury with supreme love. During the supper in John 13 He even kneels before Judas to wash his feet. Judas, a very greedy and self-centered man, was open to the devil's influence. There are still many today who reject the love of Christ. His love is clearly delineated in the cross and throughout the pages of Scripture, yet people still reject it.

The words of love that Jesus spoke drew the hearts of the other disciples to Him and pushed Judas further away. While Christ's teachings uplifted the souls of the others, they seemed to drive a stake into the heart of Judas. Everything Jesus said became like chafing shackles to him. From his fettered greed and disappointed ambition sprung jealously and hatred. In John 13:2, he is ready to destroy Christ.

F. W. Krummacher said, "Would that the traitor's kiss had remained the only one of its kind! But, in a spiritual sense, Jesus has still to endure it a thousandfold to this hour. For, hypocritically to confess him with the mouth, while the conduct belies him—to exalt the virtues of his humanity to the skies, while divesting him of his divine glory, and tearing the crown of universal majesty from his head—to sing enthusiastic hymns and oratios to him while, out of the concert-room, men not only blush at his holy name, but trample his Gospel by word and deed under foot—what is all this but a Judas-kiss with which they have the audacity to pollute his face?" (*The Suffering Savior* [Grand Rapids: Baker, 1977], p. 138). So even in the midst of Jesus' love, people still spurn Him today.

III. THE SHOWING OF CHRIST'S LOVE (vv. 3-11)

Against the dark background of Judas's betrayal, we see one of the most beautiful examples of Christ's love and one of the most interesting insights into Peter's personality. One thing we should keep in mind as we look at verses 3-11 is that love has to be more than just words. It must be acted out. John said, "Let us not love in word [only], neither in tongue, but in deed and in truth" (1 John 3:18). True love is expressed through action, not just words. Don't tell people you love them; show them your love, and you won't need to say anything.

A. The Exaltation of Christ (v. 3)

John 13:3 exalts Christ: "Jesus, knowing that the Father had given all things into his hands, and that he was come from God, and went to God." The phrase "knowing that the Father had given all things into his hands" is a comprehensive statement. Everything belongs to Jesus. Could there be anyone higher than someone to whom God gave everything? Verse 3 also says, "He was come from God, and went to

God." That's an exaltation of Jesus without equal. Christ is the highest, He came from the highest, He returned to the highest, and He possesses all that is. Why do you think John was exalting Christ here? All the more to highlight the Lord's humility. Just as Judas's hatred contrasts Christ's love in verses 1-2, Christ's exaltation in verse 3 contrasts the illustration of His humility in the verses that follow.

Christ came from God, yet in John 13, He washes the feet of His sinful disciples. That's a long step. Verse 3 shows us that the majestic God of the universe came to earth, and later we read that He knelt to wash the feet of sinful men—indescribable humility! For a fisherman to wash the feet of another fisherman is a small act of humility. But for Christ—in whose heart beat the pulse of eternal deity—stooping down and washing the feet of lowly men was the greatest kind of humility.

B. The Humiliation of Christ (vv. 4-11)

  1. The details

     It's likely that Jesus and His disciples had been hiding at Bethany during the week before His crucifixion. Prior to the supper described in John 13, they came to Jerusalem and met in the Upper Room. Their feet would have been very dirty from the journey. That was a problem faced by everyone in Israel. The roads at that time were covered with either a thick layer of dust or deep masses of mud. The sandals people wore did little to keep their feet from getting dirty. So at the entrance of every Jewish home were large pots of water used to wash people's feet. Foot washing was a slave's most menial task, and only slaves did it.

     When the twelve disciples arrived at the Upper Room, there was no slave or servant there. One of the twelve should have volunteered to wash the others' feet. Or they could have shared the responsibility and taken turns. They could have done a beautiful act of service to one another, but they were selfish. A parallel passage in Luke 22 says, "There was also a strife among them, which of them should be accounted the greatest" (v. 24). When the twelve men arrived, they were saying to each other, "I'm sitting in the first seat in the kingdom," and, "Oh no you're not!" They were bickering about who was the greatest.

When a group of people are arguing about who is the greatest, no one is going to stoop down and wash anyone else's feet. What a sickening sight the disciples must've been! They thought the kingdom was about to arrive, and they were already talking about who would be the most prominent. The pitcher, basin, and towel were all there, and everything was ready to eat. Jesus sat quietly waiting, and no one moved to wash anyone's feet. As they began eating, they were still arguing about greatness, not humility. Then He arose in a devastating act of humility to do something that must have stunned the disciples.

2. The display

John 13:4-5 says, "He riseth from supper, and laid aside his garments, and took a towel, and girded himself. After that he poureth water into a basin, and began to wash the disciples' feet, and to wipe them with the towel with which he was girded."

With calmness, majesty, and in total silence, Jesus stood up. He walked over to the pitcher, poured water into the basin, removed His clothing, and put a towel around His waist. He took off His outer robe and belt, and possibly even His inner tunic. Thus He would have been dressed as a slave. Then He knelt down and washed each of the disciples' feet. Imagine the pain and sorrow that must have penetrated the disciples' hearts! There they were bellyaching about who would be the greatest and neglecting to wash each others' feet in humility, so Jesus did it instead. That must have gripped their hearts.

I'm sure the disciples felt regret and sorrow for what they had done. None of them had taken advantage of the privilege of washing Christ's feet. They were probably brokenhearted over their pride. Christ showed the uttermost kind of love through His action. What Christ did had more impact than a lecture on humility would've had. The disciples never forgot the lesson they learned; from then on they probably had contests to see who could get to the water first. What a painful, profound lesson!

Have You Humbled Yourself?

Humility is the service of love. Unfortunately, the body of Christ is full of people who emphasize their dignity when they ought to be kneeling at the feet of their brother. The desire for prominence

127

is death to love, humility, and service. If you want prominence, you will have no capacity for love or humility. Consequently, your service is a waste. When you are tempted to think of your dignity, open your Bible to John 13 and take a good look at Jesus. There He is, clothed like a slave, washing the dirt off the feet of sinful men.

3. The dialogue

    a) The first exchange

As Jesus moved from disciple to disciple, He finally arrived at Peter, who must have been brokenhearted. He says in John 13:6, "Lord, dost thou wash my feet?" He may have pulled back his feet. Peter couldn't allow the Lord, who was the supreme One, to do such a lowly deed as washing his feet. He was convicted. Verse 7 continues, "Jesus answered, and said unto him, What I do thou knowest not now, but thou shalt know hereafter."

Jesus' response to Peter's words in verse 6 is, "You're protesting because you are ignorant." That was nothing new for Peter, He was the apostle with the foot-shaped mouth! Someday he would realize that Christ came to minister and not be ministered to. He would learn that Christ came to be humiliated. Sure enough, after Christ's death, resurrection, and ascension, Peter finally understood the humiliation of Christ. In John 13, he believes that the kingdom is coming soon, and is thinking, "Christ is the King. I can't have Him stoop to wash my feet!" But Jesus said, "Peter, you don't understand that I came to humble Myself. You'll understand that eventually; however, now you are ignorant."

    b) The second exchange

Christ's answer to Peter was gentle; He wasn't brash toward him. But Peter got bolder and said, "Thou shalt never wash my feet" (v. 8). He was essentially saying, "Cut it out, Lord!" In verse 7 Peter calls Jesus Lord, but in verse 8, he acts like he's lord. His words may seem like praiseworthy modesty, but they weren't. Obedience to God is better than self-styled worship.

Jesus' answer to Peter's second remark was, "If I wash thee not, thou hast no part with me" (v. 8).

128

Then Peter said, "Lord, not my feet only, but also my hands and my head" (v. 9). First he told the Lord not to wash his feet. But when Christ answered, "If I don't wash your feet, you have no part with me," Peter wanted the Lord to give him a bath! He went from one extreme ("Thou shalt never wash my feet" [v. 8]) to the other ("Not my feet only, but also my hands and my head" [v. 9]). That was typical of Peter.

What did Christ mean when He told Peter, "If I wash thee not, thou hast no part with me" (John 13:8)? He was saying, "Peter, I must humble Myself. That's what I came to do. I must be a servant. The washing of your feet and My death on the cross are acts of My humiliation; they are part of the sovereign plan. You have to accept My humiliation." The Jewish people couldn't accept a humble Messiah. In Peter's mind, there was no place for Christ to be humiliated. Christ was telling Peter, "You must accept My humiliation." If Peter had accepted what the Lord was doing, it would have been easier for him to handle Christ's crucifixion. In fact, by washing the disciples' feet, Jesus was preparing them to better accept His death on the cross.

Unveiling a Spiritual Truth

When Christ said, "If I wash thee not" (v. 8), He wasn't referring to washing Peter's feet but communicating a profound spiritual truth. He was saying, "Peter, unless I wash you on the inside, you are not clean and you have no part with Me." First John 1:9 tells us, "If we confess our sins, he is faithful and just to forgive us our sins, and to cleanse us from all unrighteousness." Paul said the Lord washes us with the water of His Word (Eph. 5:26). Jesus used the occasion of Peter's indignation during the Last Supper to teach that spiritual cleansing comes from Him. So not only did Christ say Peter must accept His humiliation, but He also said whoever hasn't been cleansed by Him is not cleansed at all.

No man has a relationship with Christ unless he has been cleansed of his sins, nor can an unclean man enter into the presence of Christ. In John 15:3 Jesus says, "Ye are clean through the word which I have spoken unto you." A man becomes clean only through Christ. When Christ went from the physical illustration of washing feet to the spiritual truth about the necessity of inner cleansing, Peter was still focusing on the physical illustration.

The same thing happened with other people in John's gospel: The woman at the well (John 4), Nicodemus (John 3), and the Pharisees (John 9). They all thought Christ was speaking about physical things when He was teaching spiritual truth. Because Peter thought Christ was talking about physical cleansing in John 13, he says, "Lord, wash my hands and my head; I want to be a part of You." He hadn't seen the spiritual significance of Christ's words in John 13:8.

4. The declaration

In John 13:10 we read an important statement by Christ: "He that is washed needeth not except to wash his feet, but is entirely clean; and ye are clean, but not all of you."

a) The requirement for spiritual cleansing

In verse 8 Jesus essentially says, "The only way you can be clean is if I wash you." There is no other way to God except through Jesus Christ. In Acts 4:12 Peter himself says, "There is salvation in no one else" (NASB). The only way a man can enter God's presence is when he is cleansed of his sins, and the only agency of cleansing in the universe is the blood of Jesus Christ. When a man puts his faith in Christ, he becomes clean. Since Peter misunderstands Christ's statement in verse 8, the Lord elaborates in verse 10: "He that is washed needeth not except to wash his feet."

In the Orient during Christ's time, a man would take his bath in the morning. During the day, as he went from house to house, he didn't have to take a bath each time he went into a house. Rather, he just had to wash his feet because his body was already clean. Jesus has that illustration in mind in John 13:10; He is saying, "Once you have been cleansed by the Word, all God has to do from then on is wash the dust off your feet daily."

If you're a Christian, then positionally you are entirely cleansed from sin but practically God has to wash the dust off your feet every day as you walk through the world. You don't have to be bathed all over again. We only need one cleansing because salvation is a one-time occurrence. How many times are you bathed in the blood of Christ? Once. Does that mean God never has to cleanse you of sin again? No; 1 John 1:9 says, "If we confess our sins, he is faithful and just to forgive us our sins." God keeps cleansing us. So in John 13:10 Christ is saying to Peter, "You don't need another bath. You're already a believer. You just need to get the dust off your feet regularly."

Those who are believers are purged of all sin. They are cleansed and perfected forever. If you have received Christ into your life, you are clean for eternity. Nothing will ever change that. In God's design you need only one bath; you are positionally clean from then on. All you need thereafter is a daily foot washing to cleanse your feet of the dust from the world. Every day, the precious blood of Christ keeps cleansing the dust off your feet. Christians have both a positional cleansing that is total and a practical cleansing that is daily.

b)   The rejection of spiritual cleansing

At the end of verse 10 Jesus says, "Ye are clean, but not all of you." Why did He say that out loud to the disciples? Verse 11 says, "For he knew who should betray him; therefore said he, Ye are not all clean." Jesus said what He did to prick Judas's heart. Judas knew what He meant. It was the Lord's last loving appeal for Judas not to betray Him. That's also why Jesus washed Judas's feet. Can you imagine what must have been going through his mind as the Lord knelt washing his feet? Although Christ was making an appeal to Judas, it did not deter him. He went ahead and betrayed Christ anyway. Satan had not only influenced Judas (v. 2), but would also enter into him later on (v. 27).

Jesus showed His love for the disciples by washing their feet. He also taught a spiritual truth before washing Peter's feet. He alone can cleanse men's hearts, and once you've been entirely cleansed, you only need the continual washing of your feet to remove the dust of the world. There is no cleansing apart from Christ.

IV. THE SHARING OF CHRIST'S LOVE (vv. 12-17)

A. The Inquiry (v. 12)

"So after he had washed their feet, and had taken his garments, and was seated again, he said unto them, Know ye what I have done to you?"

After Christ was finished washing the disciples' feet, He asked them, "Do you see what I'm trying to teach you?" Some people might say, "He was trying to teach the importance of His humiliation," or "He was telling them that people have to be cleansed by Him." That's true, but He taught those lessons in verses 9-11. The interlude with Peter was over, and now Christ wanted to teach the disciples a spiritual lesson: the importance of living on the basis of humility. He was not going to allow them to get away with bickering over who would be first in the kingdom. It's more important to display humility and love.

The reason Christ washed the disciples' feet was to show them how to love and serve each other in humility instead of fighting over who was the best. The lessons in verses 9-11 were just an interlude.

B. The Instruction (vv. 13-17)

1. The request for humility (vv. 13-15)

"Ye call me Master and Lord; and ye say well; for so I am. If I, then, your Lord and Master, have washed your feet, ye also ought to wash one another's feet. For I have given you an example, that ye should do as I have done to you."

The Lord wanted the disciples to do what He had done: to serve in humility. If the Lord of glory was willing to gird Himself with a towel, take on the form of a servant, and wash the feet of others, then the disciples should have been willing to do likewise. He was teaching them to serve one another. He wanted them to show love. Later on in verses 34-35 He says, "A new commandment I give unto you, that ye love one another; as I have loved you, that ye also love one another. By this shall all men know that ye are my disciples, if ye have love one to another."

How is the world going to know we belong to Jesus? There is only one way: we must show to each other the same love Christ showed to His disciples when He washed their feet. If the world doesn't realize that we're different, it's because people can't see our love. They will perceive the difference only when we love as we should.

2. The result of humility (vv. 16-17)

"Verily, verily, I say unto you, The servant is not greater than his lord; neither he that is sent greater than he that sent him. If ye know these things, happy are ye if ye do them."

Some people say they wouldn't be happy performing humble acts of service. But God said you will be happy. Do you want to be blessed by God? Learn how to serve.

Conclusion

Paul said, "By love serve one another" (Gal. 5:13). Until we are willing to do the most menial tasks with an attitude of humility, the world will not know we belong to Christ.

Focusing on the Facts

1. What is illustrated in John 13? What does Christ reveal to His disciples in John 13-17 (see p. 119)?
2. What could the Lord have been preoccupied with on the day before His crucifixion? What did He focus on instead (see pp. 119-120)?
3. Why was Christ so concerned about showing His concern for the disciples in John 13-17 (see p. 121)?
4. What is significant about the phrase "unto the end" in John 13:1 (see pp. 122-23)?
5. Mention some ways that Christ showed His love for others before His crucifixion (see pp. 123-24).
6. In what way was Christ's love highlighted in John 13:2? Explain (see pp. 124-125).
7. The more men —————— Jesus, the more He —————— them (see p. 124).
8. In what way does John 13:3 exalt Jesus? Why did John exalt Christ in that passage (see pp. 125-26)?
9. Describe the situation in the Upper Room as the disciples were preparing for the Last Supper (see p. 126).
10. What was Christ's response to the disciples' action in the Upper Room? What might have been the disciples' reactions to what the Lord did (see p. 127)?
11. If you want —————— , you will have no capacity for —————— or —————— (see p. 128).

133

12. Why did Peter initially refuse to let Christ wash his feet ? What was Christ's response (see p. 128)?
13. What spiritual truth was Christ teaching when He said, "If I wash thee not, thou hast no part with me" (John 13:8; see pp. 128-29)?
14. What did Jesus mean when He said, "He that is washed needeth not except to wash his feet, but is entirely clean" (John 13:10; see pp. 130-31)?
15. What was the main lesson Christ wanted to teach the disciples when He washed their feet (see p. 132)?
16. How will the world know we belong to Jesus (see pp. 132-33)?
17. What is the result of serving in humility (see p. 133)?

Pondering the Principles

1. Today, many people are preoccupied with self-esteem and pride. That preoccupation has even found its way into the church. As we learned in our study of John 13:1-17, pride has no place in our lives. Read Proverbs 16:18-19; Romans 12:3, Philippians 2:3; and James 4:6, 10, and summarize what you learn from those passages. Based on what you have learned, why do you think humility is such an important virtue?

2. Even though Christ was God incarnate, He was still willing to wash the disciples' feet and die a humiliating death on the cross. What does that tell you about how a leader should relate to those under him? What do you communicate to people when you are willing to serve them as Christ did the disciples? Commit yourself to following Christ's example of humility in all that you do.

3. Read John 13-17. How many instances can you find of Christ showing His love for the disciples? Discuss the different ways He expressed His love for them. Has Christ shown His love for you in similar ways? What are some other ways He has demonstrated His love for you?

Scripture Index